ALBERTA FIRESIDE GHOST STORIES

Barbara Smith

Lone Pine Publishing

Lone Pine Publishing
10145 - 81 Avenue
Edmonton, AB T6E 1W9
Canada

Websites: www.lonepinepublishing.com
www.ghostbooks.net

Library and Archives Canada Cataloguing in Publication

Smith, Barbara, 1947–

   Alberta fireside ghost stories / Barbara Smith.

   ISBN 978-1-55105-869-6

   1. Ghosts—Alberta. 2. Legends—Alberta. I. Title.

GR580.S59 2010   398.2097123'05   C2010-902201-7

Editorial Director: Nancy Foulds
Editor: Sheila Quinlan
Production Manager: Gene Longson
Layout and Production: Volker Bodegom, Kamila Kwiatkowska
Cover Design: Gerry Dotto

The stories, folklore and legends in this book are based on the author's collection of sources, including individuals whose experiences have led them to believe they have encountered phenomena of some kind or another. They are meant to entertain, and neither the publisher nor the author claims these stories represent fact.

PC: 5

Disclaimer

Although the following stories are set in specific locations within the province of Alberta, the characters and events described are strictly figments of my imagination. The stories in this book are works of fiction—and that's the story *I'm* sticking with.

Contents

Chapter 3: Full Moon

Chapter 4: Last Quarter

Dedication

For Danny—welcome to Alberta.

Acknowledgements

As always, my thanks to Shane Kennedy, Nancy Foulds, Sheila Quinlan, Volker Bodegom and Gerry Dotto for their commitment to this project, as well as to my family and friends for their love and support in all aspects of my life. But mostly I'd like to thank you, my Alberta readers. You've made this journey of mine so satisfying.

Introduction

Collecting, researching and writing the stories in the *Ghost Stories of Alberta* series (*Ghost Stories of Alberta*, *More Ghost Stories of Alberta*, *Even More Ghost Stories of Alberta* and *Haunted Alberta*) has been the most satisfying aspect of my career as an author, and it's no wonder. I've met so many interesting Albertans and have seen corners of our beautiful province that I wouldn't have if I'd followed any other path.

Those previous four books, however, have all been non-fiction, so I've been restricted to the facts as they've been told to me. Occasionally I wished that I could let my imagination leap from what I *knew* had happened, to what *might* have happened. Despite those temptations, I never added as much as a word or a thought to any of the information I'd been given, but finally with this book I've been able to indulge my urges. I'm happy to report that the experience was every bit as much fun as I'd hoped it would be.

While I find all ghost stories, real or fictional, intriguing, fireside ghost stories likely have the longest history with most of us. No one should grow up without the enjoyment of sitting around a campfire, roasting marshmallows and exchanging spooky stories. Those experiences are just too much fun to miss. It's odd, isn't it, that as long as there's no *real* danger present, being scared can actually be an enormously enjoyable feeling? Someone once told me that scary stories left her with a feeling that she loved—one she described as "being deliciously frightened." I hope that some of the tales in this collection will provoke that reaction in you.

The stories in this book are all set in Alberta. Mostly there is a ghost or two in each one, but there is also a sprinkling of tales based on other sorts of supernatural phenomena. Hopefully at least one of the stories takes place near where you live or in a place you've visited.

So now sit back, light the campfire and enjoy this spooky book of *Alberta Fireside Ghost Stories*.

1
New
Moon

The Phantom Van

"Sorry for the inconvenience," the bus driver announced to his passengers, "but I'm sure you wouldn't want me to take the chance of going any farther, not when it's the brakes that are causing the problem."

Each of the two dozen or so passengers nodded to the driver as they filed out of the highway coach.

"You'll see a small wooden building just beyond. That's actually the bus company's old office. It's not much, but at least it's shelter, and there are washrooms in there too. You should be reasonably comfortable until the garage gets a replacement vehicle to us."

Like the others, Brian Thompson nodded in acknowledgement as he stepped off the bus. Obviously he understood that the mechanical problem wasn't the driver's fault and that everyone else on board was also anxious to get to the city, but even so he didn't feel much sympathy for anyone but himself. Arlene, his girlfriend of a few months, was waiting for him in Edmonton. Working in Fort McMurray hadn't seemed so bad before he'd met her, but since they'd started dating, any delay in getting home made the distance between the two cities virtually intolerable.

Brian scuffed at the dirt under his feet and looked around. It wasn't quite 5:00 in the afternoon, but it was November and there was no daylight left in the sky. Other years a metre of snow might have covered the ground and reflected what little light there was. This year, though, had been exceptionally mild and the fields were brown; the only thing they reflected was Brian's mood.

The stranded passengers clustered together, but Brian purposely stood off by himself. He wasn't impressed with how very bad his mood was, but there was no denying it and he knew better than to try to mingle while he was feeling this irritable. Even overhearing the chatter within the knot of people made him uncomfortable, and he backed far enough away from the group that he could no longer hear them. The silence might not be comforting, but at least it wasn't as annoying as listening to the agitated voices would have been.

If only he had some way of letting Arlene know where he was and what had happened. Their relationship was new enough that he couldn't be sure what she'd be thinking—whether she'd be worried about him or mad, thinking that he'd stood her up. Neither thought improved his state of mind. Slowly but steadily he moved even farther away from the group.

The moonless evening was so completely dark that when he heard the voice behind him, he jumped.

"Whoa fella! Sorry, didn't mean to spook you," the disembodied voice continued.

Brian peered into the inky blackness. The shadowy outline of a man about his own size moved slowly toward him.

Now it was Brian's turn to apologize. "I didn't know there was anyone over here, sorry."

"It's okay. I wasn't expecting to see anyone either. Who are all those people over there?"

"Weren't you on the bus?"

"No, I take the shuttle service. They run vans, not buses. It'll be here pretty soon. There's usually an empty seat or two if you need a lift."

"It goes right into Edmonton?"

"Yeah, but it stops in Fort Saskatchewan and St. Albert first." The man paused a moment and then suddenly cussed. "I left my work boots in the bus shelter. I've gotta get them. I won't be long. Don't let the ride leave without me."

Brian nodded. He was nearly giddy with relief. St. Albert—that's where Arlene lived, so the van would be better than the bus anyway. He turned toward the people who had been on the bus. He should let them know that he wouldn't be waiting with them, but he'd no sooner turned back than he saw the outline of a full-sized passenger van pulling onto the shoulder of the road. Brian picked up his duffle bag. He wanted to make sure he got on right away. If the others spotted this alternative they'd probably all want to get on board too, and he couldn't take a chance on not catching the ride.

Brian held the over-sized duffle bag in front of him as the van came to a sudden stop, spraying projectiles of gravel, then he slid open the side door and climbed in. Much to his surprise no one from the group waiting by the broken bus as much as looked up. *Their tough luck,* Brian thought as he settled himself in the second row back. *Jeez, it's cold in here.*

"Thanks for stopping," he called from his seat. "Listen, there's another guy too. He's just run back to get his work boots. He's a regular on this route, I think. I don't know his name, but you'll probably recognize him. If you could just wait a few minutes he'd for sure appreciate it."

The driver either didn't hear him or didn't care because the van was back onto the road and picking up speed. Brian looked back toward the parking lot. There was no sign of the man who'd gone to get his boots, and the group of stranded bus passengers still appeared to be deep in conversation because no one even looked up when the van shot past them.

He nodded to the man sitting next to him but the stranger neither spoke nor stirred, nor did any of the men in the seats ahead. *They're probably all frozen stiff. It's so freaking cold in this van.* "Excuse me," Brian called up to the driver. "Can we get some heat back here?"

No answer. Brian moved forward on the seat to ask again. As he did, the van hit some uneven pavement and he had to grab onto the strap by the door to steady himself. The vinyl loop broke off in his hand, its brittle shards cutting his palm.

"What the…?" The strap might have been flexible at one time but by now was as brittle as hard plastic. Brian looked around. The seats were cracked with age and the windows were thick with grime.

He turned toward the man beside him. "What gives with this piece-of-garbage van?" he asked angrily. "The thing must be 40 years old. It's probably not even roadworthy. How does the company get away with running it? It even smells bad in here."

Silently the other man turned his head. Chunks of ice filled Brian's gut. The man's eyes were as dark as death. Brian choked back a scream of terror and lunged for the van door, pried it open and hurled himself to the side of he road.

* * *

Slowly, painfully, Brian worked his way up from the murky depths of unconsciousness. He was in a bed, that much was certain—a bed in a hospital room it seemed—a hospital room so brightly lit that his eyes, which felt as though they'd been closed for days, refused to stay open. He hurt. He hurt from head to toe. It was warm in the room, exceptionally so, he thought, and his right hand felt warmer than the rest of his body. That was his last thought before drifting back into the darkness of unconsciousness once again.

When he came awake next, the lights weren't as intense, nor was the pain, but still his right hand felt abnormally warm. It took him several minutes to realize that he wasn't alone. Someone was sitting beside him. Someone was holding his hand. Arlene—the someone was Arlene. How long had she been sitting there? Days? Weeks?

"You're awake," she said softly. "Don't try to move. I'll get a nurse."

"Wait!" he whispered with what little energy he could muster. "What happened?"

Arlene shook her head as if the mere thought of answering truthfully was more than she could bear. He held her gaze. Finally she spoke. "A local family found you. They thought you were dead. You'd stumbled down a cliff. They carried you up to their truck and brought you here to the hospital. You're badly hurt, Brian. There'll be surgeries. Your right leg is pretty bad, but at least you're still here, with us. You're alive. That's all that matters."

"More?" Brian croaked.

"No one knows much more than that. There weren't any witnesses. The only other thing I know is that you fell exactly where an old passenger van had gone off the road in the 1970s. It had been coming back from McMurray just like you were. The driver misjudged a curve and the van flew off the road into the valley below. Everyone was killed. In a way you were lucky that's where your accident happened because the people who found you had stopped there to pay their respects and to celebrate that, because of an absolute fluke of forget-fulness, their father's life had been spared. Apparently he'd gone back for a pair of work boots or something and had missed his ride."

Brain shuddered. He knew he would never explain to Arlene—or to anyone else for that matter—the circumstances of his fall down that cliff side. He watched her walk toward the nurses' station.

"Oh wait," she said, stopping and turning back. "There is one more thing. When those people found you they said you had a cracked piece of vinyl embedded way deep into the palm of your right hand. That had everyone curious."

Brian slumped back down in the bed and closed his eyes. There was a great deal he wasn't ready to deal with yet.

Heavenly Hockey

Russell was a very old man. Time had been a cruel task master, and the man's frail body and unfocused gaze belied the great athlete he once was. He was truly a mere shell of his former, youthful self. In his heyday, though, Russell had been a hockey player of some considerable consequence. Everyone always said he'd have made it right to the NHL if it hadn't been for that knee injury. And that was really saying something about a kid's talent because that was back in the day of only six teams in the league.

By now, though, people accepted that he wasn't able to do much of anything. And who could blame them for thinking exactly that? For the most part he was silent, rarely speaking to anyone but rather just spending his days sitting in his favourite rocking chair out at the old homestead west of Black Diamond.

His grandsons lived nearby, and they were good to him. In summer they'd carry the old man's rocker to the front porch. Then come winter, they'd move that same chair back inside and set it by the fireplace so their grandfather's brittle old bones could be warmed by the heat from the burning logs.

This routine went on year after year after year, but Russell wasn't nearly as idle as he appeared to be. He filled his days with the memories of his hockey career. In his mind he attended the gruelling practices, skated the killer drills, enjoyed the camaraderie in the dressing room and heard the fans roar with approval every time he scored.

To the outside world he might have seemed like an almost comatose, aged has-been, but inside his head Russ was back in his glory days, living his dream. He loved to reminisce, especially lately because he'd noticed that his former teammates were with him in those dreams more and more. He knew that all of those fellows had died; he'd been to their funerals, and that was exactly the reason he could never let on to his grandsons or anyone else that the boys came to visit him. People would think he'd gone odd in the head and of course he hadn't. He just loved to hear all about the great hockey games they were playing in the afterlife. Just listening to their tales brought the thrill of the game back to him. Their descriptions were always so vivid that Russell could feel the cold air rushing past his face and hear his skate blades scrape as they etched into the ice. He could even remember the bone-crunching hits he'd delivered in his prime—and a few he'd received. Those could still make him wince.

He certainly wasn't silent when those fellas came to visit. He always had so many questions for them. He wanted to know everything they could tell him. Is there a game tonight? Is everyone ready for it? Anyone injured? How's the ice? Is it in good condition? Who's the opposition?

Yes sir, he counted on those visits. Sometimes he'd drift off to sleep for a bit while he was waiting for them, which was exactly what had happened early one evening about the middle of February. Russell was sitting comfortably by the roaring fire his youngest grandson had built for him that morning and waiting until his former teammates could join him when, out of the corner of his eye, he saw a man he hadn't seen for decades. It was old Coach Parker! He'd been Russ's all-time favourite coach, but the man had died after just one victorious season behind the bench.

"Coach!" Russell exclaimed. "You're looking terrific. I'm honoured that you'd drop by. Do you ever see any of the fellas from the old team? Do you know if there's a game tonight?"

The older man nodded and said, "Yes, Russ, there is a game tonight, and you're in my starting line-up."

The Last Camping Trip

Greg Knight poked a broken tree branch at the bonfire he and his brother Gord had just lit. "It's hard to believe this'll be our last camping trip."

"Isn't that a bit melodramatic? I think you've been hanging around Mom too much. I'm just going away to college. I'm not dying."

"Yeah I know, but still, things will change."

Gord nodded. "They will a bit, I guess. We sure have had some good times camping in our day, haven't we?"

Greg laughed. "Do you remember that trip to the spot near Pincher Creek? It was the summer when I was about 10, so you must have been 12 or so. What a pair of nutbars we were then. We were both into all sorts of paranormal stuff."

"Jeez, I'd forgotten that," Gord said, standing up. "You were so convinced that you knew how to do the rain dance. You were dancing around the fire like an idiot for an hour until Dad finally had to tell you to knock it off."

"Oh, how embarrassing," Greg chuckled, hanging his head in mock shame as he watched his brother's overly exaggerated imitation of his childhood attempt at what he'd once seen demonstrated on tv as a rain dance. "Wait though, I wasn't the only wing-nut in those days. Remember on that same trip, you said you knew how to summon an evil spirit with eyes like burning embers?"

Gord was laughing so hard he could hardly talk. When he finally composed himself he confessed, "I just said that to scare you. I made up all that ooga-booga stuff. I remember it though—something like, 'Oh evil spirit, hear our call to you and bless us with your presence.' That was about it, right?"

"Yeah," Greg agreed. "Then when you realized how scared I was, you told me we were safe because Dad always kept the campfire going all night. You said that fire was the only thing the evil spirit was afraid of, so that would keep him away."

"Yup—we were a crazy pair of kids. Sometimes I wonder how Mom and Dad tolerated all the different stages we went through."

"They taught us a lot of things, didn't they? Even if the rain dance wasn't one of those things."

"Speaking of rain, was that thunder I heard just now?" asked Gord.

"Not a chance," answered Greg. "I checked the weather forecast before we left. There weren't any storms predicted."

"Shhhh," Gord pointed toward a nearby thicket of trees. "I don't think it's thunder. I think there's an animal or something in the bush."

As the young man spoke, the bracing mountain air turned cold and sour-smelling. A pair of red eyes moved toward the brothers' campsite as thunder crashed and the first fat rain drops splattered down. Their campfire sizzled in futile protest.

Love in the Afterlife

Ashley looked around. Nothing appeared to be out of the ordinary. Then why did everything feel so different? She knew the maze of hallways as well as she knew her route home from this theatre. After all, she'd lived in Red Deer all her life and had worked in the theatre for almost 10 years. By the time a dozen of her colleagues had walked past her like she was invisible, Ashley was not only confused but also hurt to the core.

She walked out onto the stage, sadder than she would ever have thought possible. The audience was just beginning to arrive. She always relished those moments, and today was no exception. She breathed in the energy that seemed to crackle in the air, and her heart soared when she saw the stage manager walking toward her. He was one of her favourite staff members. But he strode right up to her without so much as a nod or a smile of recognition. Worse, he didn't even acknowledge that he'd bumped into her where she stood. His only reaction was to yell out to one of the stagehands, "It's cold up here! We'll need a full house tonight to warm the old barn up!"

Ashley was fighting back tears of hurt and frustration when she turned to leave the stage and noticed a man waving to her from behind a pile of scenery, stage left. She stared at the man, wondering who he was waving at. His shoulders slumped with apparent relief when he realized that he'd gotten her attention, so she figured he must want to talk to her. *Great, of all the people here, the only one who wants to see me is a total stranger.*

"Welcome," the man said in a well-practiced stage whisper. "I'm Matthew, and I know that things seem a bit strange to you right now, but I'm here to show you the ropes, so to speak."

Ashley gave a little laugh. "No, I'm afraid you misunderstand; I'm very familiar with the theatre. I'm a performer here, a member of the troupe. I've been with this show since it started its run here. I should be showing *you* around. I've never seen you here before."

"Ashley," the stranger reached for her hand, "I'm sorry to have to tell you this, but no, you've never been here before."

Ashley shook her hand free and stared at the man as he kept talking.

"You passed over last night, just after the final curtain call. It was completely unexpected. Medically, the cause of death was an aneurysm. We would put it less elaborately—it was simply your time, and now you're here with us, on this side of the curtain."

Ashley's thoughts snapped back into what she thought was reality. "The curtain! Thank you for reminding me. It's nearly show time. The curtain will be going up."

"No, no, not *that* curtain. I was referring to the curtain of time. You've passed through the curtain of time." He paused. "Ashley, you died," Matthew told her as gently as he could.

Her head swam. She did have a vague recollection that something had happened after that last performance, but the memory was indistinct—more like a dream, the kind you couldn't quite capture the next morning. It was something about one of the performers being hurt or getting sick, that much she knew for sure. *Yes, that was it—I remember now. It was awful. There was such chaos, even an ambulance. I hate things like that. I'll have to find out who was hurt and if they're okay now. I should send flowers.*

"Come on with me, Ashley," Matthew said. "You should meet some of the other spirits here in the theatre. Most of them were quite a bit older than we were. I wasn't much older than you when I passed, though, so honestly, I do understand what you're going through. Of course, I died a very long time ago. The theatre was new then."

"What are you talking about?" Ashley stood stock still in the darkened hallway he was leading her through. "What do you mean you died? And when the theatre was new? This place is ancient. It's been here since the 1930s!"

"Yes, 1933, to be precise. I wasn't part of that first show, but I was here for a good long run in 1936. That's when I slipped through to the afterlife."

"I'm dead?" she uttered in a barely audible voice.

"Yes, Ashley. Your life ended last night, but you'll be all right. Today is the first day of your afterlife, and believe me, it's even more fun than life. Being dead has lots of advantages."

"What about my poor parents and my brother? They must be devastated." The reality of her situation was beginning to sink in.

Matthew lowered his eyes. "They are for now, but they'll feel better in time, and there are things you can do to reassure them. I can show you some of the tricks we use to contact the living, but not just yet. You need to give everyone a chance to get used to your death. For now, would you like to see the show? It's about to begin."

Ashley tried to smile, but her body felt so different that she wasn't sure it had worked. "I'd like that. Where shall we sit?"

"I see two empty seats in the first row of the balcony. Would that suit m'lady?" Matthew said with a broad grin and a wink.

Ashley nodded. Before she could speak they were seated. The show was fun, but even as a cast member she'd known that. She missed the wonderful rush of adrenaline that performing always shot through her veins. She stole a look at Matthew. There was something tremendously appealing about him. He had a kind face.

After the show, the two beings contentedly watched as the living members of the audience left the theatre. Ashley laughed when Matthew pointed out that they didn't have to stand up to let people get past them and out into the aisle.

"Did you like seeing the show?" he inquired.

Ashley nodded.

"Want to go for a cup of coffee or a drink or a bite to eat somewhere?"

"I'd like to go and see my parents, Matthew. If they're half as worried about me as I am about them, I couldn't enjoy being out having fun with you. If I could just let them know that I'm all right..." her voice trailed off.

"It's too soon," Matthew said quietly. "Trust me on this. I've been dead for many years and I've watched lots of people pass over. Maybe next week we'll check on your family. For now they need time to adjust, and so do you. Please take my word on this."

He paused to let her take in the information. *She's so pretty. I hope I handle this well. I don't want to scare her off. She just might be the one for me—the one I could spend my happily ever afterlife with.*

He tried to sound especially cheery as he explained that she'd enjoy meeting the other spectres in the theatre. "But those introductions can wait. For now, let's just have fun. What would you like to do first? Scare someone? Move at the speed of light? Time travel?"

Ashley found Matthew's sense of fun contagious. "Let's scare someone," she giggled before adding, "Oh, but just a little. We don't want to really terrify anyone, do we?"

"Of course not. Something that really works well is just letting a person know we're here. That always gives them food for thought. Let's go out to the street. We'll find plenty of people there."

No sooner had Matthew said they'd go outside than they were there. Ashley had no recollection of leaving the theatre; it just happened. She was still taking in the scene around her when she noticed Matthew already getting up to some tricks. As a well-dressed, distinguished-looking lady walked by, he lifted her hat from her head—just for an instant—and then put it right back. The victim's air of sophistication vanished as she twirled around, muttering exclamations. Ashley and Matthew laughed.

"Try letting people walk through you. That's fun too," Matthew suggested.

"How on earth do I do that?" Ashley inquired.

"Well, the fact that you're not really on earth anymore helps considerably. Stand still beside me. See those two walking toward us? They can't see us. Let's see what happens."

As the humans walked straight through the two frolicking phantoms, the man pulled his jacket a little closer around his body and the woman commented absently, "I wish I'd worn a sweater under this coat."

"See," Matthew said. "It's fun!"

Ashley smiled, and this time she was sure her smile showed. She took Matthew's hand. He sighed happily, knowing that he'd finally met his soulmate.

The Devil Wears Armani

Joanna was more than a little surprised to find herself walking eastbound in the alley behind Whyte Avenue. The popular Edmonton neighbourhood was one she knew well and visited often, but normally she walked on the sidewalk in front of the stores, not in the grungy alleyways behind them. She never thought she'd be relieved to see one of the area's shabby-looking homeless people, but there was no one else around and if she could at least find out what time it was then she might be able remember what had happened. She called out to the man.

He heard her. She was sure of that, but his only response was to slam the heel of his hand against the side of his head before turning and shuffling away with what seemed to be as much haste as he could muster.

Weird, Joanna thought. *I guess alcohol really isn't good for a person.*

Oddly, that thought jarred the shadow of a memory loose. She recalled being out for dinner with Bradley and two of his stuffed-shirt government friends. They had wanted to leave the restaurant. She hadn't. As far as she was concerned the night was just getting going, and she'd told Brad that in no uncertain terms. That was her last recollection of the evening.

Joanna turned south toward Whyte Avenue. The fog in her head lifted just a bit. *I must look a sight,* she thought, and glanced toward her reflection in a store window. *How wild is that? No reflection. The window must have some kind of coating on it.*

At the intersection ahead, a man in a business suit waited for the light to change.

"Excuse me, sir. Could you tell me the time?" Joanna asked, stealing an admiring glance at his Armani suit.

The man in the expensive clothes turned toward her. "That's not important now," he said, and, dropping the newspaper he'd been carrying, he reached for Joanna's arm. "I've been waiting for you."

Confused, Joanna glanced down at the newspaper the man had dropped. *Well, look at that. My picture's on the front page. I certainly didn't look a wreck when that was taken. Brad must have done something big for my picture to be in the paper. He'd better not have resigned. The perks of this life are too good.*

But then Joanna looked at the headline: "Politician's wife in fatal traffic accident. Alcohol a factor. No charges laid against driver."

In a flash her memory flooded back. She'd stumbled out of the restaurant hours after the others had left. She'd been hailing a cab…

She looked down. A long, bony hand protruded from the beautifully tailored suit.

"You need to come with me," the devil said.

Cross-time Skier

"Looks as though you're having a bit of trouble. Anything I can do to help?"

Startled, Valerie swung around to the direction of the man's voice, almost losing the precarious balance she had on her narrow cross-country skis. *I must have been concentrating so hard on trying to repair this strap that I didn't hear him ski up to me. I don't suppose the "stranger danger" applies here because if I don't get this binding fixed before dark, I'm hooped.* "Yeah, I do need some help," she admitted. "Thanks for stopping."

It was the first time she'd looked up from her ski in over 20 minutes. She was surprised to see how little light there was left in the sky. When she realized it was already so dark that she could barely make out the man's features, she was doubly grateful that he'd happened along. She wouldn't have had much time left before nightfall. Out there after dark, alone on the trail—way too scary to even think about.

"No problem," he said as he released his silver skis and pushed the fur-lined hood on his parka back a bit.

Valerie glanced over hoping to see a trustworthy face smiling back at her, but all she could make out was that he had a neatly trimmed beard and was wearing big, kind of awkward-looking glasses. Judging by his voice, though, her knight on shining skis was neither a very young, nor a very old man. *I'll pretend he's just like my dad,* the young woman told herself.

"I see what's happened here. The pin on the buckle clasp is bent. If you can shuffle your way just over to that cabin," he said, pointing, "I can straighten it out with a pair of pliers."

"Do you think it'll take long to fix? I shouldn't have left the lodge. My parents were busy with my younger brother and I just took off. No one knows where I am—they'll be worried about me."

"Come on," the man beckoned. "We can talk at the cabin while I'm fixing the buckle. It's just over there a way."

Mutely, the girl followed along beside and a bit behind her alpine Good Samaritan. *I'm glad none of my friends can see me pushing myself along like this. I must look like some kind of a geek,* she thought.

"You're here with your family, are you?" he asked as he held open the door to a cabin that she hadn't noticed before. It was warm and welcoming inside.

Valerie nodded in response to his question. "We're kind of touring a few of the lodges around Lake Louise to see which one we like best. The plan is to spend Christmas at our favourite. It's a fun trip, but I just really needed some time on my own."

"I know exactly what you mean," the man acknowledged. "I came here with a group of friends. They all wanted to stay back in the chalet, but I needed to get some fresh air and clear my head. Good thing, too. If I hadn't come out, there might not have been anyone on the trails to help you."

"It's a lucky coincidence for me. My mother always says there's no such thing as a coincidence, though."

"Well, I'm just glad everything worked out as well as it did. And," he said, setting the ski back on the floor, "there you are.

You'll need a new binding, but this will get you safely back to the chalet, anyway."

"Thanks," Valerie said with concern back in her voice. Her ski might be reliable now, but the sky was completely dark. How would she find her way back to the resort? Her poor parents would be beside themselves with worry by now.

"Come on then. I probably know this area better than you do. I'll ski with you back to the lodge," he offered.

Tears of relief and gratitude stung her eyes. *I hope my parents do something really nice for this guy,* she thought as she planted her ski poles and pushed off to catch up with the man.

They hadn't been skiing for very long when Valerie glimpsed lights in the distance. *That must be the hotel,* she thought. *I wasn't as far out as I thought I was. Still though, I sure couldn't have made it on only one ski.* "I can take it from here," she called to the man. "If you want to get back to your cabin I'll understand, but if you could spare a few minutes I know my parents would want to thank you for stopping to help me the way you did."

When the man didn't answer, Valerie looked all around. He was gone—nowhere to be seen. She was alone on a snow-covered field. "Huh?" she asked her empty surroundings.

Then, in the silence that followed her one-word question, Valerie was sure she heard someone calling her name. It was her mother, standing on the hotel patio calling out for Valerie in a panicked voice.

"I'm here! I'm here, Mom!" The young woman waved her arms frantically before digging her poles in as hard as she could to help propel herself toward the warmth of a loving hug.

"Valerie! I'm so glad to see you. We were worried. Your father will be relieved that you're all right," the older woman fussed as she hugged her daughter tightly. "And the rest of the hotel staff too. They were about to send a search party out for you."

"I'm sorry to have worried everyone, Mom. It was awful. Or it would have been if this man hadn't stopped to help me. My binding broke just as I was turning around to head back here. I'd already stayed out a bit too long anyway, then the strap snapped, and while I was trying to fix it the sun disappeared behind the mountains. It was getting so cold and so dark."

"A man stopped to help you?" her mother asked. "Where is he now? Where did he get to?"

"That's just it, Mom. I don't know. He skied with me to where I could see the hotel, and then when I looked, he was gone."

"You weren't out with those boys from the room down the hall, were you?"

"No, Mother, I wasn't. I'm telling you the truth. Look, you can see where he's bent that little piece of metal in the binding on my left ski."

"I can," the older woman agreed. "I'm sorry, I should've known better than to question you. Come on. We need to tell the others that you're all right."

As the pair made their way into the lodge they were met by the hotel manager, who used his two-way radio to call off preparations for the search and arranged for Valerie's father and brother to be given the good news.

"How ever did you find your way back in the dark?" the manager asked.

For the second time, Valerie began to explain her chance encounter with the mysterious skier.

"Did he have a beard?"

Valerie nodded. "And he was wearing glasses—big ones—sort of old-fashioned looking."

"Is this the man who helped you?" The manager lifted a framed photograph off a nearby table and passed it to the young woman.

There, with the small cabin in the background, stood a group of skiers. The third figure from the left was definitely the same man who had helped her less than an hour ago. He even had on the same parka with the fur-lined hood.

"That's him!" Valerie all but squealed with delight. "Mom, we have to do something to say thank you to him. I hate to think what could've happened to me out there if he hadn't come along and offered to help."

But before her mother had a chance to say a word, the lodge manager spoke again. "I think you two had better sit down," he said. "You might be a little shocked at what you're about to hear."

"That man isn't some sort of criminal, is he?" Valerie asked. "Could he have hurt me?"

"Let me explain, as best I can," he said, slowly shaking his head from side to side. "As best I can figure, the man who helped you was Eric Shaw. I'm absolutely sure he was never a criminal, and I'm even more positive that he couldn't have hurt you. Shaw was a scientist. Many years ago, he and a group of his friends stayed at a small cabin near here. He was trying to work out a particular problem with an experiment he'd been working on. He told his friends that he needed to get some fresh air to clear his head so that he could think.

They tried to convince him to stay in because it was getting dark out, but the man was determined. He wanted desperately to find the solution."

"Yes," Valerie interjected. "He told me that he'd gone out that afternoon without his friends because he needed some time on his own."

"Well yes, in fact he did go out by himself that afternoon, but 'that afternoon' was more than 20 years ago. You see, he skied off the main trails and into an area that the groomers had roped off because they were concerned about the stability of the snow. The staff's worry was justified, it seemed, because Eric Shaw was buried in an avalanche."

"That's terrible," Valerie said with evident concern. "How did he ever dig himself out?"

"That's what I'm trying to tell you, Miss. He didn't. Dr. Shaw died instantly." The hotel manager took a deep breath before finishing his explanation. "His ghost, however, seems to be determined that no one else will ever lose their life in the snow in this area."

The Souvenir

For the sixth time in less than an hour, Doug looked at the clock on the bedside table. It was nearly 1:00 in the morning and he was tired. People had warned him that it was tough to get any sleep in the town of Peace River during the month of June because the sun shone for all but a few hours each night, but despite the relentless daylight he'd had no trouble falling asleep the previous three days. This was his last night away, though, and maybe he was more anxious to get home than he'd realized because he simply couldn't quiet his mind.

Hoping that a cigarette and a bit of a walk would help him relax, Doug got out of bed and pulled on some clothes. Outside, the warm twilight air felt good. Obviously summer's long days and short nights didn't cause the townsfolk any trouble sleeping because he noticed with some envy that the streets were deserted.

Doug had been surprised at how very much he'd enjoyed his stay in the northwestern city. Usually he didn't fare too well being away from home, but this trip had been different. He'd never seen the Mighty Peace before, and its grandeur had left him awestruck. Lighting a cigarette, he walked to the middle of the bridge crossing the river. The powerful current of water flowing under his feet was a sight to behold.

A solitary man walked slowly toward the bridge. Doug might not have noticed him at all except that the man was wearing a sports jacket—which seemed odd considering the time of year and the temperature.

"Evening," the man said as he approached.

Doug nodded silently in response.

"Don't suppose you could spare one of those?" the man asked, indicating Doug's cigarette.

Doug reached into the pocket on his t-shirt and held the open cigarette package toward the stranger. The man took the cigarette almost greedily, as if he'd been without nicotine for longer than was comfortable. As he stood closer, it was clear that he didn't look well. He didn't seem drunk or stoned, but he looked shaky, as if life hadn't gone his way for a while. He certainly didn't appear to be any sort of a threat, though, and it wasn't like giving up a cigarette or spending a bit of time chatting was going to interfere with anything Doug had planned. As a matter of fact, a conversation would be a welcome diversion for 15 or 20 minutes.

"Got sent up here from Rocky Mountain House. My boss wanted a job site checked out before he bid on the project. Been here since Monday, but I fly out late tomorrow—I guess technically today, now," Doug said, looking over at the man. There was something oddly compelling about the stranger's appearance. His eyes were red-rimmed and sunk deep in their sockets. Maybe the extended daylight hours had given him insomnia too. His clothes were clean and good quality, or at least they had been at one time. Now they were frayed and worn-looking.

"Do you have a souvenir of your time in Peace Country?" the stranger asked.

Doug laughed. "I'm not much of a souvenir collector, actually."

"I have something here that might interest you," the man said, reaching into his jacket pocket.

For a moment Doug was apprehensive. He couldn't have a gun, could he? But no, it wasn't a gun he pulled out of his pocket, it was just a piece of paper—a very old piece of paper, judging from the looks of it. The man's hands were shaking as he held the sheet toward Doug. A stylized drawing of a bear took up most of the piece of paper, but someone had also made detailed notes around the drawing.

"Let me tell you the story behind this," the man continued. "It's only a copy, but even so it's worth something because it's a good copy. I know it's good because I did it myself. It took me weeks—and that's precisely why I might as well give it away. You see, I'm a forger. Counterfeiting, that's been my career for more than 20 years, and it's served me more than adequately but, well, you saw my hand twitch when I held it out. I've started to shake something awful, and that's the kiss of death in this trade. If a forger's going to be of any use to anyone, he has to be quick and he has to be steady. I'm neither by now. What I am, frankly, is scared. There aren't exactly good pension plans in my line of work."

Doug was taken aback by the man's honesty. It must have had something to do with the weird setting they were in—the middle of the night and broad daylight, on a bridge in a town where they were both strangers.

The man's story also piqued Doug's curiosity. "If it's a copy then why does it look so old? And what's it a copy of?"

"Creating convincing-looking aged documents is a necessary skill for a counterfeiter. It used to be one of my specialties."

Doug looked down at the brittle, slightly discoloured paper he was holding. The simplicity of the drawing was undeniably attractive. Matted and framed, hung in the hall by his front door at home, the unusual drawing would be a real conversation piece. Yes actually, he did want it—copy or not.

"What's it a copy of?" he asked the man.

"You've heard of the native carver Elmer Rider? He lived most of his life in a cabin just west of town here. He died 50 or more years ago now, so his work goes up in value every year as more people get to see and appreciate his artistry with soapstone. He always did a detailed sketch before he started a carving. Then as soon as the sculpture was complete he'd burn the sketch."

"I remember reading about that. Rider died before he could complete his last work. It was the most ambitious work he'd ever taken on. Am I right?" Doug asked.

The man nodded. "No one's ever finished the bear, of course. It's on display here in the town's museum. The drawing's there too. That's how I was able to practice my skills on it. The people at the museum must've wondered about me—sitting there for hours staring at a piece of paper, but it was something I needed to do. I had to find out if I still had it in me. Sadly, I don't, but I guess I knew that day would come eventually."

"I'd like to give you something for your work," Doug told the man, "but I don't have any money with me."

A look of relief crossed the man's face. "I wouldn't take anything for it. I'm starting fresh. Please, let this be my first transaction since retiring from the life of crime."

"Are you going to be all right?"

The man didn't acknowledge the question, and silence hung in the air between them for a moment. "Best of luck to you," the man said.

"You too," Doug replied, but the man didn't hear. He'd already walked away into the gathering darkness.

Back in his motel room Doug stretched out on the bed. If he could fall asleep right away, he'd still be able to manage five good hours of sleep before the alarm clock rang. If he couldn't, he knew he was going to feel dreadful trying to function in the morning. And he knew which way this one was going to go because he was even more restless now than he had been before he'd taken the walk and talked to the strange man. He had put the small drawing away. The paper was so fragile and the drawing itself so faded that it was hard to believe it had just been made this week. The stranger's abilities as a forger certainly impressed Doug, but he was not the audience that those skills needed to impress.

He tried to go over the conversation he'd had with the man, but he was distracted by how uncomfortable he was getting. It was suddenly freezing in the room. *How the heck did that happen?* Doug wondered.

He began to shake, violently. *This is ridiculous. I hope I'm not getting sick.*

He got up to splash water on his face. That usually made him feel better, but when he saw his face staring back at him in the mirror he gasped in horror. He looked dreadful. Years had been added to his face in less than an hour. He was pale. His eyes were red-rimmed and sunk back in their sockets.

A rancid smell filled the room. Doug swung around toward the door. Someone was watching him, he was sure. But of course that was ridiculous. There couldn't be anyone watching him because there was no one else in the room.

Then what was that shadow in the corner? A cool breeze brushed past his back, as though someone had just walked behind him—but they couldn't have—he was leaning against the bathroom sink. Heavy footsteps plodded across the floor above him—except that there wasn't a floor above him.

The motel was only one storey high. He jammed his fist in his mouth to keep from screaming.

"Give my drawing back," an angry male voice hissed.

Doug lunged for his suitcase and pulled out the piece of paper. He ripped a corner off as he grabbed it, but what did that matter? He had to find the man who had given the drawing to him and give it back. Never mind the plan for the frame and the front hall. That was a dumb idea anyway.

The shadow in the corner of the room was growing and deepening. Almost running, Doug fled from the motel room and headed for the bridge. If the man was still there he could give the cursed drawing back to him. But the man wasn't there. He was nowhere to be seen. Didn't matter. He was getting rid of the paper. Doug grabbed the cigarette pack from his shirt pocket. In a panic he shook the last of the cigarettes onto the bridge deck and stuffed the drawing into the empty package. Then he jammed his lighter in on top of the paper for weight and threw the horrible bundle into the Mighty Peace.

There, it was gone—whatever it was.

With an unsteady gait, Doug shuffled back to his motel room. By 5:00 that morning he'd finally fallen into a fitful sleep. An hour later the alarm clock rang, and he felt worse than he could ever remember feeling. He needed to get home—soon, very soon, as soon as he possibly could.

The desperation he felt must have been evident in his voice because the reservation clerk who took his phone call at the airline didn't question Doug's request or mention anything about change fees. She switched his booking from the evening flight to the first one out in the afternoon, and Doug was at the airport well ahead of the time she'd specified.

He went into the washroom but averted his eyes to avoid looking in the mirror. He didn't want to know that he still had that haunted look.

He thought of buying a magazine for the flight but decided against it. He didn't think he'd be able to concentrate on anything. The trouble, though, was that it would seem like an awfully long flight if he didn't have something to distract himself with. A newspaper, that's what he'd do. He'd pick up a copy of the local newspaper.

There, on the front page, was a photograph of the drawing Doug had thrown into the river. The man's story had been a lie. That wasn't a copy. It was the original, stolen the day before from the city's museum. Police presumed that the thief had been trying to get the priceless, unfinished, last work of Elmer Rider, but a security guard had interrupted him and the man had fled. A poorly made copy of Rider's working sketch had been dropped near the sculpture. The original, which was kept on a shelf beside the exhibit, was missing.

A weight crushed in on Doug's chest. He lurched back to the men's room, pushed open a stall door and leaned against it while violent shakes ricocheted through his body.

If only he didn't understand the consequences of what he'd done. But he did. He'd destroyed an invaluable artifact and angered the spirit that possessed it. How much damage—and to whom—had he caused?

When his flight was called Doug made his way toward the gate, his legs so unsteady that moving them required conscious effort. He had never been so anxious to be home.

The Favour

Ted sat up in bed so suddenly that he was upright before he was awake. *What the…? What woke me up?*

As his eyes began to adjust to the darkness, Ted thought he saw an odd shape over by the window. Was someone in his bedroom? There was a strange smell too. He could smell flowers. Adrenalin surged through his body. *What's going on? Maybe I'm still asleep. Maybe I'm dreaming. I'm not, though.*

The only sound was his heart pounding against his rib cage—until the shape by the window spoke. "Ted," a whispery, barely audible voice said. "Don't be afraid. It's only me—Grandma."

"Grandma? What are you doing here? Mom said you're in Florida."

"I was, but I couldn't settle until I let you know something."

Ted shifted uncomfortably in his bed, not sure about what might be the polite thing to do. After all, his grandmother had come a long way to see him and it would've been nice to greet her properly, but he didn't think the older woman would appreciate seeing him in his boxers. Fortunately, he seemed to be the only one concerned about the odd situation because she just kept on talking.

"You know the cabin at the lake? I need you to do me a favour and get something from there. It's at the very back of the last drawer in the kitchen. This is important, Ted. You need to find it."

He stared toward the darkened shape. He recognized his grandmother's voice, but the room was especially dark in that corner and he wasn't able to make out his grand-mother's features.

"Ted?" she said sharply. "Are you paying attention to me? You need to listen. This is important."

"Yeah, Grandma, I'm paying attention to you—the junk drawer in the kitchen at the lake, right? I'll get you whatever it is you need from there, but you have to be a little more specific. That's where everyone throws stuff."

Ted noticed that although the sun was starting to rise and his bedroom was now perceptibly lighter than when he first woke up, he couldn't make out the dark shape in the corner of the room by his window anymore. He looked around, wondering if his grandmother had moved to a different part of the room.

"Grandma?" he called in a stage whisper. "Grandma, are you still there?"

Ted rubbed his eyes and looked again. The shadow in the corner was definitely gone. He switched on the lamp beside his bed. His grandmother was nowhere to be seen.

"I must have been dreaming," he muttered to himself before turning off the light and immediately falling back into a deep sleep. By the time the alarm clock rang three hours later, he had forgotten about his middle-of-the-night visitor. Instead he had urgent financial matters on his mind. Today was the day he would have to give his notice to the obnoxious new landlord who had bought the plaza where he had his bike repair shop. The guy just wanted to flip the building and turn a quick profit; that much had been obvious from the minute he'd given Ted the ultimatum. He could either pay the new rent rate—fully twice the amount it had been—or buy the building—his choice.

It had taken Ted a year to turn a profit, but by now the business was growing. Buying the building would have been great, but if he couldn't afford the new rent he certainly couldn't get a down payment together. The only thing he could do was clear his equipment out of the shop and let people know he was shutting down the business.

Usually Ted felt a sense of pride when he unlocked the door to the shop in the morning, but today there was none of that good feeling, only frustration, anger and disappointment. He looked around the cavernous room. He hadn't taken in any new work the week before because he knew there was no point. His business didn't have a future.

"Screw this," he informed the empty building. "I'm getting away for a while."

A few minutes later the young man was driving toward Lac Ste. Anne, where his family had owned a cabin since the 1950s. It wasn't a place he would have gone to if it hadn't been for his rotten mood. He'd never particularly liked the cabin. It had always seemed cold and unwelcoming to him, so he usually avoided being there by himself. *Just shows what kind of a dumb, funky mood I'm in; I know the place is empty this week.*

Ted pulled off the road and onto the lane leading to the small, clapboard cottage. He walked up the steps and across the porch to an oversized ceramic frog. He knew the key would be under the frog's left foot. No one had been near the place for several weeks, so it would be stuffy inside. It was also cold inside, he quickly discovered. He propped the door open and went back to the truck to get his jacket. Given the mood he was in, he probably wouldn't have remembered that his cell phone was in the windbreaker's inside pocket, but the distinctive stuttered ring was hard to ignore. It meant that

New Moon 45

he'd missed a call but that whoever had called had left a voice mail. *Probably that stupid landlord,* he thought, punching in the code to retrieve the message.

"Ted? It's me, Mom. You need to listen," his mother's voice instructed. "Are you paying attention? This is important. You need to phone me as soon as you get this message."

Funny—I never realized how much her voice sounds like Grandma's. Reasonable, I guess, they're mother and... Ted's thoughts trailed off. Grandma! Beads of sweat formed on his forehead. He'd had some kind of a weird dream or something that his grandmother had been in his room during the night. That was just stupid, though, because he knew she was in Florida. But it wasn't just his mother's *voice* that sounded similar to his grandmother's in that dream; she'd even said the same things: "This is important" and "Are you paying attention?"

Was that a dream? Now that he remembered his conversation with the older woman, it didn't feel like a dream at all. *Grandma really was in my room. She told me to look for something in the junk drawer,* he remembered as he hurried into the kitchen, pulled the end drawer out and dumped the contents onto the counter. Nothing—nothing aside from the things that everyone who was too lazy to put in their proper place had left.

He picked up an assortment of the detritus and dumped it back into the drawer. That's when he noticed an old, yellowed paper taped to the upright at the very back of the drawer. The tape had peeled away at the edges, but enough of the glue held that the sheet hadn't fallen when he'd turned the drawer upside down. Ted eased the tape free and opened the folded paper. On the top right hand corner was his name, and under it, his birth date. Puzzled, he realized that he was holding a life insurance policy that his grand-mother had bought for him the day he was born.

"Too weird," he muttered to himself as he hit memory dial to return his mother's phone call. "Mom? I got your message, what's up?"

"Ted, I'm so glad you called back. I just heard from Bess, your grandmother's friend in Florida. I'm sorry to have to tell you this, but Grandma died last night."

A Local History

Fred Baxter shifted self-consciously from foot to foot. Everyone else in the drama club wanted to do *On Golden Pond* for this year's Paintearth County Theatre production, but Fred had his own agenda. As a budding playwright he was seriously hoping to get the group to change their collective mind.

"Any amateur theatre company anywhere can do *On Golden Pond*. We have a chance to be a lot more original than that. I've been looking into a piece of local history that's as dramatic as all get out."

"You can't be serious, Fred. Nothing even a little bit interesting has ever happened in this town," Mabel Brown called out derisively.

"She's right and you know it," shouted someone else over the murmurs spreading through the room.

"Hang on a minute, folks!" Bernie Phillips called out over the din. "There might be something in what Fred's saying. Let's at least show him the courtesy of hearing him out."

Silence hung in the room for a few awkward moments before Mabel mumbled apologies, and a few other people urged Fred to explain himself. He cleared his throat unnecessarily and began to speak.

"When I was a kid growing up here, there was a story around town, almost an urban legend. The tale seems to have faded into obscurity by now, but in those days telling and re-telling that tale was an important rite of passage for the teenagers, usually about the second year of high school."

"Do you mean the one about those deaths that one summer?" a woman asked.

"I do, Nicole. That's exactly the story I mean. It's always intrigued me, and I think it would make a compelling play. As a matter of fact, I'm convinced enough that it'll work that I'm willing to spend my evenings and weekends for the next couple of months writing it."

"If Fred's willing to invest his time like that then I think the least we can do is see what we think when he's done explaining," the ever-diplomatic Bernie commented, and the crowd nodded its approval.

"Excuse me," a woman's voice called out from the back of the room. "I'm new to the area, so I don't know the story. Can you give me a bit of a run-down on what the play would be about?"

With only the slightest nod to acknowledge the question, Fred launched into the tale.

"The setting is right here in this town, but a good while ago—back about 1936, which would probably explain why you won't hear it told very often anymore. There are three main characters, and everything takes place during one day. I'd tell each character's story separately and then tie them together in the final act."

At that point Fred relaxed a bit. He could feel that he'd captured everyone's attention, and he knew this was the perfect opportunity to make use of his story-telling skills to make his case. "It was a typical, sunny, Alberta summer's day," he began.

Soon his audience forgot they were listening to a man talking. He told the old legend so well that each person in that room could see the story being played out in their mind's eye.

They clearly saw Helen Lange, the Spinster Lange, as many folks called her, contentedly tending the flower gardens around her little house when a shadow suddenly fell across the patch where she was weeding. The sun was blocked out so entirely that Miss Lange might have wondered if a sizeable cloud had come out of nowhere—except that this shadow had a distinctively human shape.

Startled, she looked up expecting to see one of her neighbours standing beside her and to hear the person apologize for having frightened her. But that was not what Helen saw or heard, and for just a moment, she thought she might faint dead away for there, standing not two metres away from her, was Ralph, the man to whom she'd once been engaged.

"Ralph, could it be you?" Helen whispered as she scrambled to her feet and struggled to stand on legs weakened by the emotion of seeing the only man she'd ever loved, the man she'd hoped to spend her whole life with, the man who'd been killed in France at the Battle of Vimy Ridge on April 10, 1917.

As Helen reached out to grasp the man's hands, his image vanished as mysteriously and suddenly as it had appeared, leaving behind a dreadful chill where the apparition had been.

Devastated, she ran into the house to tell her mother what had happened. Shocked and concerned, the older woman had her daughter lie on the couch with a cold cloth on her head until the doctor could get there. His diagnosis was sunstroke. He recommended rest and cool fluids for the next 24 hours.

That same afternoon at the high school just three blocks away, Stan Jones, Helen's nephew, was late getting to biology class. The door to his locker had jammed closed. He'd worked at it for 15 minutes before he finally managed to pry it open, and then 10 months' worth of papers, old lunch bags, binders and textbooks slid down around his feet. He was crouched on the floor, shoveling the detritus back into the inadequate metal cupboard when, just his luck, who should stroll by on hallway supervision but the principal.

"Get that locker cleaned up before you do anything else today, Jones," the man bellowed.

Stan sighed. He knew better than to argue with the principal, but tidying his locker with just a few days left in the school term seemed like a waste of time. The chore took him a lot longer than the break between classes lasted, so Stan was alone in the school hallway outside the science lab when he suddenly sensed a presence beside him. Figuring that one of his buddies had managed to slip away from biology class and had come to find out what had happened to him, Stan opened his mouth to call the principal a foul name.

But something made the boy look up before he spoke, and when he did he was glad he'd remained silent because there, standing in front of him, was his grandfather. He had died the previous year.

"Gramps?" he asked incredulously, blinking hard in an effort to make sure his eyes weren't playing tricks on him. After the third blink, the image of his grandfather was gone as surely as it had been there.

Later when Stan tried to tell his friend about the incident, he remembered that as soon as his grandfather's image appeared, the hallway had turned icy cold.

A rustle ran through the people listening to the story.

"Fred," an elderly man in the group called out. "I know about this incident first hand. I'm the friend he told."

"Well, Tom, then you can attest to the fact that this isn't merely an urban legend but is, in fact, a verifiable piece of our local history."

Tom nodded solemnly as Fred continued.

"As best anyone can figure, at the same time Stan and his aunt had those strange experiences, Daniel Baker, the town's pharmacist, watched as an old-fashioned hearse all draped in black stopped at the big Thompson house across the street from his drugstore. Two exceptionally small men stepped out of the hearse and scurried up the steps of the big old place. The scene was so odd that Mr. Baker left his dispensing area and ran to the front door of his pharmacy. He didn't recognize either of the men, nor had he ever seen a hearse like that. It certainly didn't belong to Mr. Connelly, who owned the funeral parlour just off Main Street. But by the time Baker was out of his store, the strange vehicle and its equally strange occupants were gone, leaving no trace that they'd ever existed.

"That evening was the first night of a home stand for the town's ball team. Local baseball was a really big thing in those days, not just in this town but all across the prairies. Just before the game was about to begin, Stan and his aunt, the Spinster Lange, were helping Stan's mother at the food concession beside the bleachers at the ball park. Before the game began, John Thompson, a World War I veteran, stood at the pitcher's mound to salute the flag while a recording of 'God Save the King' was played. That was how things were always done around here in those days.

"They say it was a beautiful day, not too warm, just a few puffy white clouds in the sky and a mere cat's paw of a breeze. At the second line of the anthem—the part about 'Long live our noble King'—a dark, oddly shaped cloud formed over the centre of the infield. Thompson screamed once and then ran away from the mound, all the while looking back over his shoulder. Some players ran out to catch him, but they were too late. He ran headlong into the concession booth. He sent the deep fryer flying off the counter. Boiling fat poured out, scalding both Stan and his aunt Helen. Stan died instantly. Helen lingered for a few days before she succumbed."

"What about John Thompson?" the newcomer asked. "Was he burned too?"

"Not a speck of oil on him," Fred answered.

"So not all three of them were killed then?" the woman persisted.

"No," Fred explained. "Thompson wasn't killed as such. He died of a massive heart attack. That's what caused him to lunge against the counter and knock over the deep fryer. No one knows what caused him to charge off the field like that. The strangest part of the whole incident is that some folks who were there, some of the town's most reliable citizens, swore to their dying day that they saw two exceptionally small men chasing John Thompson."

For a moment, silence hung in the community hall as Fred finished his description of those tragic events that took place in 1936. A few seconds later a ripple of applause and cries of "yes" spread through the meeting room.

The play was a huge success when it was performed the following season. Its popularity even led the drama club to create a tradition of presenting plays based on local history.

Love Is Where You Find It

The grain elevators are gone now—more's the pity—but the town remains, and a wonderful little place it is. As a matter of fact, if this charming village isn't the pride of southern Alberta then it certainly should be. The townsfolk are not only as friendly and hospitable as can be, but they're easy-going too—definitely not the sort to take themselves too seriously.

There's a particular story about this place that's as special as the town itself. The tale begins just after the towering grain elevators near the coulee at the edge of town had been decommissioned but not yet demolished. Of course, everyone had known that closing day was coming. It was simply an inevitable, but bittersweet, result of progress.

Not long after the operation shut down, word spread that a local vagabond named Joe had set up temporary housekeeping in one of the abandoned elevators. No one minded in the least. As a matter of fact, people seemed pleased to think that the old place was serving such a good cause. Of course those same folks had no idea of how well placed their benevolent thoughts were, for the hobo appreciated his stay at the elevator more than any of them would ever know.

The first time Joe saw the presence in the elevator was a night when every board in the drafty old tower moaned pitifully in the strong prairie winds. He'd bunked down in empty elevators many times before, so the creaks and groans didn't disturb him at all. He was sitting quite contently daydreaming in a corner when a movement across the room caught his attention. He fixed his stare into the darkness. When he couldn't make anything out he shook his head to clear his mind just in case he'd been sleeping, even though he knew he hadn't been. He hadn't been drinking either, so the unexpected motion couldn't have been caused by moonshine.

But there it was again. There *was* something moving! Near the far corner of the room, a column of grey mist hovered just off the floor.

The wispy vapours weren't frightening, but they were confusing. Given the number of blessings that had *not* been bestowed on Joe at birth, confusion was a familiar state for the man and so not in the least worrisome for him. After a few moments he drifted into a deep, dreamless sleep. By morning, the fact that he'd seen a cloud moving in a grain elevator had left his mind entirely.

At dusk the next night, though, a sudden chill in the dusty air of his makeshift home did capture his attention. The elevator walls were quiet, so wind billowing up from the coulee couldn't have caused the sudden drop in temperature. Shivering, Joe looked around his empty surroundings for a solution to the uncomfortable problem, or at the very least an explanation for it. And that's when he saw the smoky column for a second time. Only then did he remember having seen the image the night before.

The cloud of mist wafted slowly toward the man, bringing its chilly ambience with it. Joe's face and hands were icy cold, but he didn't mind because the closer the strange shape came to him, the warmer his heart became. If the man had ever in his life felt love then he might have recognized the sensation he was experiencing, but he hadn't, so he had no word to describe what he was feeling. He just knew it felt good, indescribably good. After that night, the good-feeling cloud came to the elevator and spent every night with him.

When Joe went into town to beg for food, people noticed that he was looking better than he had in years. They presumed that the change in the homeless man's appearance was because he was living closer to town and therefore wasn't as isolated. And, in a way, they were correct. Some folks worried about what would happen to him when the elevator was torn down.

The day the men and equipment arrived to tear down the elevators, the entire town turned out to watch the demolition. The buildings were so old that very few people could remember a time when they hadn't been there, and as the people gathered they began to exchange various memories they had of the prairie institutions. One old fellow recalled the cold, heartless agent who had been assigned to their area back in the Dirty Thirties. No one in town liked him, but everyone, it seemed, liked his wife and felt sorry for her. Esther was her name, the old-timer remembered. When folks realized that they hadn't seen her around for some time, they asked the elevator agent where she was. He told them she'd gone to visit her sister in Saskatchewan, but frankly, no one believed him.

It was about then that people began to complain about feeling uncomfortable when they were anywhere near the elevators. Once the bad-tempered agent retired and a new person took over the stories died down, but even so, no one ever found the elevators a pleasant place to be—no one until old homeless Joe, that is.

As he left his elevator for the last time, just a few minutes before the wrecking ball took its first swing at the old wooden towers, people commented on how changed he was.

"It's as though something's breathed new life into him," a woman commented.

"Oh, I don't know about that," the woman's husband countered. "Look at him, poor guy. He must think there's someone walking along beside him. The way he's smiling and nodding, you'd swear someone or something was talking to him."

And so the tale began when the elevators were decommissioned, but no one knows when it ended—or even if it's ended yet.

Be Careful What You Save

During the 1920s, the Crowsnest Pass in southwestern Alberta was a busy place. Coal miners were mining coal and rumrunners were running rum. A certain man, whom we'll call Romeo, had become very wealthy through dealings in both of those enterprises, and his unexpected death one winter's day created a potentially profitable situation for a man engaged in a third local industry—undertaking.

When Romeo's son Hiram brought his father's body to the undertaker's premises, the younger man gave strict instructions that his father's remains were to be treated with the utmost respect. Everything to do with his burial had to be of the highest quality. Toward that end, Hiram even supplied the lumber so that his father's coffin would be built from the very best material. "I want you to use all of this wood to make my father's casket," the grieving son explained.

But, once he was alone with the corpse, the undertaker realized that if he skimped just a bit here and a bit there he could make a perfectly adequate coffin and still have enough lumber left over to make a lovely book shelf for himself. No one would ever be any the wiser, he was sure.

The man carefully inspected each piece of wood he'd been given and set aside the very best one for his own project. Then he hurried to start making the coffin. The sooner he could get Romeo's body out of his shop, the better. Even though he was well used to working with the departed, for some reason this particular corpse was making him decidedly uncomfortable.

That evening when the undertaker went to bed he had trouble falling asleep, and when he finally did sleep he slept badly. Nightmares of the corpse shouting accusations of thievery at him tormented the world inside the man's mind while a snowstorm ravaged the world outside. The wind's fury dashed sheets of ice pellets against his windowpanes. In his dreams, undulating silhouettes whispered messages to him, but, try as he might, he couldn't quite make out what the dark shapes were saying. He woke up suddenly in a cold sweat, sure that it had been Romeo's spirit that had disturbed him. He jumped from his bed and lit the lamp that stood on a nearby table. The light flickered three times before dying out completely, and no matter how hard he tried, the undertaker could not get the lamp's wick re-lit. Soon he gave up entirely and hurried back to the warmth of his bed. An unbearable chill had permeated the room.

The next morning the undertaker was surprised that he felt well—not even a bit tired. He took advantage of his unexpected energy by finishing the last bit of work he had left to do. Then he laid the body in the coffin he'd crafted from almost all of the wood he'd been given for the job and stood back to admire his handiwork.

He was pleased. Hiram would never guess that the casket his father's body lay in was missing one piece of lumber: the best piece.

The snowstorm that had blown in the night before continued to swirl mercilessly throughout the Pass. The undertaker knew that even though he desperately wanted to get Romeo's body out of his shop, it would be foolish to try to make the delivery while such a storm raged. Instead he decided to spend his time building the shelf he'd been wanting. That would keep him distracted until the storm eased enough that he could travel. He was desperate now to deliver the body that lay in the next room.

As the undertaker worked away, the sounds his tools made seemed to be eerily whispering to him.

"Foolish man," the chisel hissed. "You'll live to regret your theft."

"Die," the vice groaned as the man tightened its clamp.

An inhuman, mirthless cackle echoed throughout the dingy room.

He spun around to see where the voices were coming from. Panic overtook him and he could no longer even *think* of waiting until the storm had subsided before getting the bedevilled body out of his quarters. He loaded the coffin onto the wagon that served as his hearse, hitched up his old nag to her harness and started down the deserted, snow-covered and wind-whipped road.

The next morning the town's grocer found the undertaker's overturned wagon. The horse had broken free of its reins and run off, perhaps in terror, because its master's body lay dead beneath the remnants of the casket. Beside him lay Romeo's body, a sardonic smile frozen on its ice-blue lips.

Table for Four

Karen, Veronica and Heather had been getting together on the second weekend in June every year since high school graduation, when career paths had taken their lives to different corners of Alberta. Their annual reunion always began with Saturday brunch at a particular restaurant in the pretty, centrally located city of Red Deer.

At least, that's how it went every year but one when, for some reason, the restaurant didn't have a record of their reservation. Veronica blamed Heather, who vehemently denied being at fault. Karen, always the positive one in the group, suggested they create a moveable feast by simply trying another cafe. Somewhat grudgingly, her two friends agreed and soon they were seated at a table in a less-crowded diner.

The views from the windows here weren't quite as nice and the ambience wasn't nearly as special, but, as Karen pointed out, being seated at a table for four meant they had an empty chair where they could put their purses. Veronica and Heather clearly weren't listening to her, though, because they each tucked their purse on the floor at their feet.

"Isn't this quaint?" Karen asked as she followed her friends' lead and set her purse down on the floor beside her right foot.

"'Quaint' isn't quite the word I would have used," Veronica offered.

"'Dumpy' describes it better, I think," Heather added.

"Oh come on, you two. Where's your sense of adventure? Just look around you; there must be a hundred years of history in this building. Did you see the gorgeous old black and white photos in the lobby? Wouldn't you love to have seen this area by the river years ago? The scenery must have been breathtaking."

If the other two women had planned on responding to Karen's time-travel premise, their intentions were interrupted by a tired-looking, middle-aged waitress with menus. Once their meals arrived, conversation was reduced to just a few words between mouthfuls, and even those were awkward because the small restaurant was, by then, busy and noisy.

"Who else is up for dessert?" Veronica asked, mere seconds after the three women had finished their entrees. Without waiting for her friends to answer, she raised her hand to signal to their waitress. Seconds later a middle-aged woman approached the table, but it certainly wasn't their waitress. She wore a little felt hat set back on her tightly curled hair, gloves and a long, nondescript coat. Much to the friends' surprise, this decidedly odd stranger sat herself down on the empty fourth chair.

The three young women looked quizzically at one another but picked up their conversation as best they could, partly out of amused embarrassment at the woman's mistake and partly to give the intruder as many clues as possible that she was at the wrong table.

Veronica looked the other way and tried, once again, to signal to their waitress. Heather and Karen followed their friend's stare in case one of them caught the eye of any staff person at all. After a time, they gave up entirely and brought their attention back to their table. When they did, they were surprised to see that the older woman had settled herself quite comfortably in their company.

"Maybe I'll forego dessert after all," Veronica said.

"Let's check into our hotel," Heather suggested as they all stood up. "I'll just freshen up a bit before we leave," she added while they walked toward the restaurant door.

"Can't you wait until we're at the hotel?" Veronica asked with an edge in her voice.

"No, frankly I can't," Heather replied, smiling sweetly and pushing open the swinging door marked "LADIES."

"This place gives me the creeps. I'm going to wait outside at the car," Veronica announced, leaving Karen in the darkly panelled foyer covered with framed black and white photographs. Many of the pictures showed groups of men dressed in old-fashioned clothing. Some were in chaps with cowboy hats while others were wearing bowler hats and string ties. A few had on wire-rimmed spectacles. But it wasn't the men in these pictures that interested Karen. In two of the photographs there was a woman—a very familiar-looking woman. She wore a little felt hat set back on her tightly curled hair, gloves and a long, nondescript coat.

This is the woman who came and sat down at our table, Karen realized with a shock. "Excuse me," she called out to a man behind the cash register.

Seeing that Karen was staring at the wall of pictures, he nodded. "Those old photographs are great, aren't they?"

"Yes, but…"

"Life was tough back then, especially for the women, I think. That's my great-grandmother. Apparently she ran this place single-handed after her husband died. Couldn't have been easy, but she endured. Rumour has it she haunts the place, but of course that's a crock. Everyone knows there's no such thing as ghosts."

When Heather came out of the washroom, Karen grabbed her arm and held tightly to it as the two friends made their way out to the parking lot where Veronica was waiting for them.

Throughout the entire weekend Karen kept her ghostly secret, so when the three friends bid each other farewell, the other two couldn't possibly have known how completely sincere Karen was when she told Heather and Veronica that it had been a weekend she would never, ever forget.

Dancing Bride

Once upon a time, just outside Picture Butte, a beautiful baby girl was born. Her parents had waited a long time to have a child, and they treated their daughter like a princess.

She was probably the happiest child in the entire province. As she grew up it became obvious that the girl was not only beautiful and fortunate but smart too. So it was that after high school she enrolled at the University of Lethbridge, where she met a handsome young man. The two quickly fell in love. Her parents were delighted with the turn of events in their daughter's life and quickly arranged for their princess to be married in a castle that stood at the edge of a small town in the Alberta Rockies.

The morning of the ceremony, workers at the castle scurried about in preparation so that every detail would be perfect. The bride's gown was so white it glowed, and her elegant train flowed gracefully and shimmered as she walked. This would be the perfect wedding, her mother knew as she watched the workers carefully place tiny white candles on each step of the circular staircase where her beloved princess-daughter would descend later that day.

At the appointed time, guests who had come from miles around gathered at the foot of that delicately lit staircase to watch the fairy-tale nuptials. When the door at the top of the stairs opened, a gasp echoed through the group. No one had ever before seen a bride of such exquisite beauty. Holding her proud father's arm, the young woman began to make her way slowly down to where her beloved waited for her.

The train of her bridal gown swept elegantly across the curving staircase, dangerously close to the candles that glowed at the edge of each step. Seconds later, the guests gasped again, this time in horror. The bride's train had brushed up against a candle's flame and had caught fire. Terrified, the young woman pulled away from her father, lost her balance and fell to the bottom of stairs at the feet of her horrified groom. She died instantly.

Instead of a wedding that day, there was a funeral the next day. The grieving guests left the castle, and the groom was never himself again.

Many years later, employees at the castle, which was not really a castle but a palatial mountain hotel, began to report seeing a column of glimmering white vapour at the bottom of the resort's circular staircase. The mist is always said to be the height and shape of a small human being, and it moves in a graceful, rhythmic fashion just a little above the floor.

Those who have seen the phenomenon say that although the image is indistinct, it's utterly captivating. And that's really no surprise because it's generally believed that the vaporous mist at the bottom of the staircase is, in fact, the spirit of that long-ago bride dancing the wedding waltz in death that she never got to dance in life.

2
First
Quarter

Going Up

Carolyn jumped aboard the empty chairlift as it whirred its way around the gate. *I was smart to pick this lift instead of the new quad,* she thought, looking down at the line-up for the larger, and supposedly faster, ski lift. *That one might be faster once you get on, but there must be a 20-minute wait for an empty spot.*

Sliding her ski-suited bottom to the back of the metal chair with practiced proficiency, the young woman held her ski tips high and settled in to enjoy the trip up the mountainside near Banff. As she looked around she noticed that there was a skier on the chair directly behind her. *Well, isn't this just my lucky day? Not only do I get on the lift without having to wait in line, but the only other person riding it is a very cute guy!*

"Hi there," she called enthusiastically in his direction. Her inventive mind was already creating plans to waste a few moments at the top of the run until his chair came around, then make a little conversation, perhaps ski down the slope with him and maybe even pop into the chalet to get to know one another over a mug or two of hot cider.

But the young man didn't acknowledge her greeting. He didn't even seem to have noticed that he wasn't alone on the otherwise deserted ski lift. *Maybe he couldn't hear me,* Carolyn thought as she waved instead. *I'm doubly glad now that I chose the pink ski suit. He might not have been able to hear me, but he can't help but see me waving.*

When she didn't attract his attention that way either, Carolyn had to admit to herself that she was slightly miffed. *Maybe he's one of those snobby types who thinks he's too good for everyone else on the slopes. All the more reason to wait and ski down with him. I might be a bit sore from that wipe-out I took this morning, but I'll bet I can still show him a thing or two about plowing through powder.*

The mechanism on the old lift creaked mightily as it pulled the cables around the top of the run. Carolyn slipped off the chair effortlessly and glided out of the way. She watched intently as the next chair rounded the apex and the young man she'd been admiring from afar slid to a spot not three metres from her.

"Hi there," she repeated with what she suspected was more enthusiasm than appropriate.

Despite being only a few metres apart and the only two humans within sight of each other, the young man didn't acknowledge her greeting. As a matter of fact, he still acted as though she wasn't even there.

Embarrassed by the increasingly awkward situation, Carolyn responded in the way she always did when she was ill at ease. She began to chatter.

"We were smart not to get sucked into waiting in line for that new lift, eh? I'll bet we can make two runs before half the people in that line-up are even at the top. We'll beat them, and they don't even know they're in a race. Speaking of which, I'll race *you* to the bottom," she dared the silent young man who was staring off into the distance. "Loser buys hot chocolate for the winner. Sound fair?"

But before the young man found the courtesy to answer, he turned away from her and toward the edge of the slope. Skillfully, purposefully, he began to ski down the side of the mountain. As he reached the chalet at the bottom he took a deep breath.

"Bruce!"

He turned in the direction of the voice. His friend Michael was heading toward him.

"Hey, Mike," he mumbled, wondering whether or not to say anything about the experience he'd just had. *Maybe not,* he decided, unsure as to whether he would even be able to describe the shimmering, pulsing, dark pink cloud of sparkling light he'd seen floating on the chair ahead of him.

"Hey, Brucey-baby. Where ya been? We've been looking all over for you. Have you tried the new quad-lift? Man, is it fast. They're shutting the old one down for good tonight. It's time they got rid of that creaky old thing anyway. It's creeped me out since I was a kid and my older brother's stupid friend told me that it was haunted. There was supposed to be the ghost of a girl dressed in some bright psychedelic colour from the seventies who always dared guys to try and ski with her. Of course, the punchline of the story was that if you took her up on the dare, you'd die too."

Bruce had been standing beside a snowdrift as his friend spoke, and that was a good thing. Otherwise he could have hurt his head when he fainted.

Special Service

Jane and Edward lived in a little frame house at the edge of a churchyard not far from Devon. Over the years they had become creatures of habit and took great comfort in their routine.

An important part of that routine was a visit from their children and grandchildren every Sunday afternoon. The elderly couple devoted that entire day to their cherished guests. They always spent Sunday morning preparing for the young people's arrival, Sunday afternoon enjoying their visitors and then Sunday evening reflecting on how much they'd enjoyed their company.

Jane and Edward also liked to attend church services regularly, which made living right next door to the church a great advantage, and the fact that there was a Saturday evening service made that part of their comforting routine very simple. Nowadays they didn't have as much energy as they'd had when they were young, so as a matter of course, they'd be sure to have a nap late Saturday afternoon. They would wake up refreshed and then fix themselves a bite to eat just before the service at the church was scheduled to begin.

As soon as Jane and Edward heard the chapel bells ring at 7:00 on Saturday evening, they would put on their coats and make their way together across the yard to the church. After the service was over they liked to dawdle a bit and visit with the other members of the congregation, but Jane especially was very conscientious about not lingering too long. She always insisted on being back home comfortably before midnight.

One Saturday afternoon, both Edward and Jane felt exceptionally tired, so they went for their nap a little earlier than usual. Despite the early start to their rest, they slept late and didn't wake up until Edward heard the church bells chiming the announcement that the service was about to begin.

"Jane dear," he said leaning over and gently shaking his wife awake. "We've slept in. Do you think we can manage through church without supper?"

The elderly woman had been in the deepest sleep of her life, and it took a few minutes for her to come fully awake. Once she did, though, she agreed that they could manage without eating and added that they should leave right away in order to be in church for the processional.

It was darker outside than the couple had expected it would be, but they didn't have far to go so it didn't much matter.

"We really are late," Jane told Edward as they made their way up the church steps. "Everyone else has gone in. We'd better be extra quiet and just take a seat in the back pew. People will already be settled. We don't want to disturb anyone."

Edward nodded and held the door open for his wife, but the woman had barely stepped over the threshold when she stopped dead in her tracks.

"Edward!" she said in a stage whisper. "There's something wrong. That's the old minister at the pulpit."

Edward looked around his wife and into the church as best he was able. "Can't be," he replied. "That man died last year. We went to his funeral, don't you remember?"

Jane and Edward were now standing in the church vestibule. All the pews appeared to be full. "Maybe we should just go back home," Jane suggested, her voice rising with concern.

But by then, the couple's whispered conversation at the back of the church had disturbed the congregation. Everyone had turned around to see who the latecomers were.

Jane gasped at the sight of the familiar faces. She recognized every one of them. These folks had all been their friends in days gone by, but each one of them was dead. "Edward, we've missed our regular service. This is why I never wanted to linger too long on Saturday evenings. It must be midnight, the time the dead come to pray."

By now the people in the congregation had left their seats and were coming toward the back of the church to greet Jane and Edward. In spite of a strong feeling that they were somewhere they weren't supposed to be, the couple was delighted to see all their old friends again and hurried forward to embrace them.

The next day their children and grandchildren found the elderly couple in bed. Death had taken Jane and Edward that Saturday afternoon during their pre-church nap. The couple died as they had lived, peacefully and together.

A Grave Real Estate Error

The early 1970s were exciting years in Alberta. The economy was booming, and it seemed that everyone had jobs—jobs that paid extraordinarily well. It was then that Natasha met Paul.

Maybe they weren't exactly made for each other, but they were both young and completely caught up in the fun of making lots of money. Life was terrific, and they were sure that it would stay that way forever. They figured that the only way their lives could get any better would be if they were to get married and buy a house. And so they did.

Their wedding was a lavish affair at an exclusive golf club on the outskirts of Calgary. Shortly after their honeymoon in Hawaii, Natasha and Paul went house hunting. By now they'd both become very used to having everything exactly as they wanted it, so they agreed that only a custom-built house would do. When they found a builder planning a community just west of the city, they knew they'd found the perfect location. They were excited to be the first buyers in the subdivision because it meant they had their choice of lots. The views from the land they chose were spectacular—so spectacular that at first, they drove out every weekend to the spot where they would soon be living.

Then a particularly severe Alberta winter set in, and the drive became a chore. Just thinking about their new dream house became irritating because the builder hadn't as much as started to dig its foundation. But by this time quite a few things about their life together were starting to irritate both Natasha and Paul. Even so, they were sure that once they were living in their beautiful new house everything would go back to being perfect. The trouble was, it didn't.

When the new house was finally ready and they had packed their things in their downtown apartment, Natasha was surprised to realize that she felt sad. She tried to tell herself that she'd love the peace and quiet of the suburbs, but in her heart she knew she'd miss the hustle and bustle of the city. Paul, however, was really anxious to move. He'd been getting more and more cranky about the noise downtown, and Natasha figured moving would be worth it even if all it did was shut him up. His constant complaining was starting to get to her. She'd certainly had no idea when she married him how negative he could be.

Moving day dawned clear and warm. Paul left to pick up the rental truck while Natasha organized last-minute items. A few hours later they arrived in their new neighbourhood—except that it didn't seem like a neighbourhood at all. They could see their house the moment they turned off the main road because it was the only one finished. The streets were so covered in mud that Paul had trouble steering the truck. Natasha yelled at him to be careful and he yelled at her to keep quiet—which she did, until a few minutes later when they stood in the foyer of their dream home and she announced, "Something feels weird about this place."

"You are not going to ruin this for me, so just shut up, okay? I was afraid we'd never get out of that noisy apartment. I hated it there. Look, if we work our butts off we can have all the furniture in here by suppertime. Frankly, I can hardly wait."

It took until well into the evening, but eventually the rented moving truck was empty. They fell into bed exhausted but more pleased with themselves than they had been for many months. Moments later they were both asleep.

Unfortunately, Natasha didn't stay that way. An hour later she was wide awake, sitting bolt upright in bed, clutching the covers to her chest and gasping for air. She had no idea what had wakened her; she just knew her heart was pounding in terror. A reassuring hug would have helped a lot, but waking Paul up just didn't seem wise. *I must have had a nightmare,* she thought, getting up to splash water on her face.

Boxes were strewn all over the bedroom, but moonlight shone through the uncovered windows and she was able to find her way to the bathroom easily. She paused to stare out the window. *How can Paul think this is so beautiful?* she wondered, looking out at the barren landscape surrounding their house. *Stop moaning,* she told herself. *It won't be empty for long. We should have neighbours in no time. That house across the street is already framed, and the foundation has been dug out for the one next to it. It'll feel like a real community soon.*

Reassured, Natasha went back to bed promising herself that by morning she'd feel better—about everything.

And she might have too, except that she couldn't stay in bed. Something drew her back to the window. As she stood there shivering, the scene outside morphed hideously. Moonbeams slanted ominously through the skeleton of the framed house across the street. Next to it, the grave-like excavation yawned a lazy welcome. The spine of surveyor's stakes pounded into the oozing quagmire led to the few twig-like trees the builder had been required to plant. Their barren, boney fingers pointed menacingly—at nothing.

Something doesn't want us to be here, she thought, sliding to the floor. There she stayed, waiting for dawn to bring light and reason to her isolated, evil-feeling world.

Natasha awakened sitting where she'd huddled down hours before. Rubbing the grit from her eyes she stood, her back to the window. She had no desire to even glance at the ominous scene outside.

Paul sat up in bed and asked, "Wasn't that the best sleep you've had in years?"

Natasha could only stare mutely while she tried to collect her thoughts.

Paul continued, "I'm going to get dressed and take the truck back to the rental office right away. You stay here and unpack, all right?"

A few minutes later, as she stood on the makeshift front walk of their new house and watched her husband drive away, a shudder ran through her body. Nervously she rubbed the toe of her sneaker against the edge of the mud-caked stone she was standing on. An odd shape appeared. Natasha bent down and wiped more of the dirt away.

There were words written on the roughly laid stone— words and numbers. The young woman's screams echoed uselessly in the emptiness as she realized the implications of her discovery.

She was standing on a gravestone.

Phantom Moon Rider

Winter nights in southern Alberta's ranch country are silent and silver-white, lit by millions of tiny stars in an immeasurably high sky. The world is devoid of colour and so still that it might also be equally devoid of people.

The December night that Aaron Slater set out on his journey to a neighbouring ranch, he felt as though he was the only human being in the world, and the fantasy pleased him. Tomorrow he would be the best man at his brother's wedding. He was looking forward to the celebration, but chores had kept him on his own property long past the time he'd hoped to have been with his family. It was fully dark by the time he left home, but Aaron didn't mind. He was an expert rider and on the best mount he owned. The ride between the two properties would be swift and exhilarating.

Cold air cut at his body as the horse galloped ever faster. Aaron couldn't remember ever feeling more alive. Adrenalin coursed through his veins, and he concocted primal fantasies that delighted him. Suddenly he knew that Vivian, the woman of his dreams, loved him with superhuman passion. He would confess his love for her when he saw her the next day. The timing was perfect, for she was the bride's maid of honour. He urged his steed on.

The gleaming white snow and ice, lit by the moon and stars, cut a bright swath across the frozen landscape. He rode on surrounded by a solitude that felt strangely like loving companionship. The wind blurred his vision. He blinked in a vain attempt to erase an ethereal image of another horse and rider galloping in unison—neither out of sight nor quite within his sight. Without so much as a conscious thought, Aaron knew that what he was sensing wasn't real. His mind was playing tricks on him. The image didn't even cast a shadow. Even so, he spurred his horse on to escape the mirage. He'd never speak to anyone about the uncanny illusion his strange surroundings had created.

The image of the other horse and rider didn't seem to accelerate, and yet in a gale of ice crystals, the presence forced past him at an unearthly speed. Who could this rider be? Aaron was confident in his horsemanship. Few, if any, riders could keep up with him, let alone lead him. He drove his horse even harder, just trying to keep up. Getting to his brother's was no longer the goal. Now his compulsion was to pursue this phantom rider over the frozen landscape and through the dense forest circling the lake he'd intended to cross.

As he cleared the last of the trees he pulled his horse up sharply. The spectre of the other horse and rider was nowhere to be seen. It had simply vanished. Aaron leaned forward to pat his horse's neck in appreciation for the animal's amazing speed and endurance. He loosened the reins and let the horse trot the last kilometre.

Relieved to have made the enchanted journey safely, Aaron let himself into the welcome warmth of his brother's home. The other man sat hunched in a chair near the door. He barely looked up as Aaron came toward him.

"Why so sad? You should be celebrating, brother! Tomorrow's supposed to be the happiest day of your life."

"Supposed to be. Yes. It *was* supposed to be," the man answered.

"What do you mean?"

"There'll be a funeral tomorrow, not a wedding. Vivian died today. She'd been out riding with my bride-to-be and led them on a path across the lake. The ice was thin in a particular area and the horse went through. She managed to pull herself out of the water, but she only lived for a few minutes after that. Her last words were of you. You never told me you two were together. Did you know that she loved you?"

A River Runs Through It

Frank Chapka waited and watched. He'd chosen his resting spot on the hillside for its panoramic view of the fast-flowing river, but the bushes around him meant it was also an effective hiding place, and he was free to be utterly absorbed by the scene before him. A woman, probably a few years younger than he, dressed in an old, cheaply made housedress, grasped a trowel and was scraping at the sloping ground. Her reward for this tedious diligence stood nearby—a metal bucket full to the brim with coal chips.

Frank had lived in Edmonton all his life. Like far too many of the city's men, he was now suffering the effects of the Great Depression. For the past three years he'd relied on government handouts to keep a roof over the heads of his wife and daughter. They had managed so far, but the strain of it was wearing on them all. His moods lately varied from lethargy to desperation.

Now though, watching the woman scavenging on the riverbank had given him something he hadn't had for many months—hope. Through Edmonton's long, brutally cold winters it often felt as though spring would never come. Paying for coal to heat their frame house had been a matter of course when Frank had been employed, but being on relief made even such necessities as heating fuel seem like luxuries.

As he watched, the industrious woman nearby stopped to rest, likely realizing that she had as much coal as she could carry. She set her trowel down, got to her feet and lifted the heavy pail. A second later Frank Chapka jumped out from his hiding place.

"Give me that," he demanded, startling the woman. The freshly mined coal they both wanted spilled out on the ground around her.

The woman knew better than to fight for what was rightfully hers. She hadn't heard from her husband since he'd gone looking for work the year before. Even if he was still alive it was obvious that he wasn't coming home. That meant that she was the only parent her three children had. Coal veins were plentiful on the banks of the North Saskatchewan River. She could get more another day, but she couldn't risk her life. Without her, little Jesse and the twins were as good as orphans. She turned to flee.

"Wait!" Frank yelled, feeling oddly confused and angry. When he'd left the house that morning he hadn't expected to find an easy source of heating fuel. Then, when he had, he hadn't expected the woman to give up her bounty so easily and run. His gut churned and heaved. It was ridiculous, but he was hurt that she was afraid of him. He didn't like to think of himself as frightening. He was also irritated that now if he wanted to take the coal home he'd have to gather the black chips that lay scattered about on the sloping ground.

"Wait!" he repeated, and lunged toward the woman. He grabbed the hem of her dress. The flimsy fabric ripped. She lost her balance. A second later he watched and listened as she fell head over heels down the hill, screaming until her head struck a rocky outcropping. Then her screams stopped—forever.

Panicked, Frank scrambled up the hill toward Jasper Avenue, stopping a few metres short of the wooden sidewalk to catch his breath. The woman was most certainly dead. The angle of her head told him that, even from a distance. Her body would be discovered soon. If someone remembered seeing him in a panic near where the body lay, there were sure to be suspicions.

Self-discipline wasn't one of Frank's strengths, but he did manage to reign in his urge to run. He slowed his pace and calmly walked the few blocks north on 96th Street to his home. With every step he tried to erase the afternoon's events from his memory.

That night, visions of the woman, her dress ripped and her face bloodied, tormented his sleep. Her image hissed unintelligible words at him. By morning the awful dream, if in fact it was a dream, had repeated itself a dozen times. He wasn't able to make out what she was saying, but Frank clearly understood that the woman he'd killed was threatening him.

The next day the words "...sins of the father..." echoed in his head over and over again. Soon he was sure those were the words the spectre had spoken. The self-centred, cowardly man didn't dwell on the horrors he'd created but only on the apparition's implied threats of retaliation. *What have I done?* he wondered, remembering the chilling whispers through the night and the echo of the phrase "sins of the father" throughout the day. Would the woman's spirit harm his dear daughter? He couldn't bear the thought.

That evening, the local radio station carried a report about a pair of 10-year-old boys who had stumbled across a body in the river valley. One of the boys had been especially traumatized by the grisly discovery because he recognized the dead woman as a neighbour whose husband hadn't been seen for some time. The dead woman's children had evidently spent the past night alone. They would be sent to foster homes and, the newscaster added, as it was unlikely any one home would take all three children, they would have to be separated.

For Frank, the most important part of the radio report came at the end. The doctor who examined the body declared that she had died as a result of a fall. Police found evidence that she had been working a gopher hole mine and surmised that she had lost her balance on the hill while carrying a bucket of coal. After talking to the woman's neighbours and learning that she didn't have an enemy in the world, police ruled out foul play and closed their investigation.

Frank breathed a self-serving sigh of relief. He didn't, however, forget the horrifying visions he'd had through the night nor the words of warning that they'd imprinted on his subconscious. He watched over his daughter very carefully as she grew into adulthood.

Much to his relief and astonishment, the girl seemed not to have been cursed in any way. Perhaps more amazingly, she apparently hadn't inherited even one of her father's despicable qualities. As a matter of fact, as the years went by, the only reminder Frank had of that deadly day by the river was a foolish tale that would occasionally be told about a ghost in the river valley. It was said that there was one area near the bottom of the hill that stayed especially cold all the time, even when the rays of the summer sun fell directly on it.

Fortunately, Frank had never believed in any sort of ghost, but even if he had, this one had to be the figment of some-one's imagination because he noticed that the description of the phantom changed over the years. At first the tales described the manifestation of a woman no more than 30 years of age, but the last time he'd heard the story, the ghost was an old crone. It was absurd to think that ghosts existed at all, let alone that they aged as the years went by. Besides, what did it matter? Those terrible visions he'd had right after the altercation obviously hadn't been premonitions because his daughter had turned into a lovely young lady who'd recently married a fine man and was about to make Frank and his wife grandparents for the first time.

When the baby boy was born there wasn't a prouder grandpa anywhere. Despite his daughter and son-in-law's protestations, Frank spoiled little Harold at every opportunity. By the time the lad was a teenager, he was so used to getting anything and everything he wanted that no one could control him and few had any fondness for him. His behaviour was breaking his mother's heart, and she asked her father to talk to him. "You're the only one he might listen to," she pleaded.

The next day Frank suggested that he and the boy go for a walk. Thinking that his grandfather was once again going to slip him some money, Harold quickly agreed to the plan. Once the two were strolling along the well-worn path on the bank of the river, though, it was clear that this walk with his grandfather wasn't going to be as profitable as others had been in the past. Harold was angry and disappointed. He knew he'd have to win the old man over, but he'd done that before and so knew exactly the way to do it—by doing something nice for his mother. Usually it didn't take too much to smooth things over. As a matter of fact, he was sure that he'd seen something that would serve exactly that purpose—a small bouquet of flowers sitting on the slope just a few metres away. That would make everyone happy. "You're right, Grandad. I'll take Mother some flowers. I see just the ones," the young man said, trying to sound contrite.

He climbed off the path and up the hill toward the posey he'd spotted. With every step the temperature in the air around him dropped. By the time he reached the spot where the flowers lay, he was very anxious to be back where it was warm. Oddly, the flowers seemed to have been purposely placed in the particular spot where they lay. They were in a small vase that had a note taped to it. "This spot and these pretty flowers are sacred to my grandmother's memory. How I wish I'd known her," the card read.

"Dumb thing," Harold muttered. Shivering, he pulled the flowers out of their holder and tossed it aside. The vase rolled down the hill, not stopping until it had shattered against a rocky outcropping. A second later, the boy crumpled to the ground.

No one ever knew for certain what had caused the seemingly healthy teenager to collapse and die that day. And really there were two lives lost because it was said that Harold's grandfather, Frank Chapka, never recovered from the tragedy of losing his grandson.

The only intelligible words the older man ever spoke after that day were an odd phrase, something about the sins of the fathers....

A Night Beyond

"Getting to a bush party at Lac La Nonne was hardly the reason Mom and Dad left us the car, you know. Why don't we wait until morning and meet everyone for breakfast at Smitty's like we usually do?"

Lindsay sighed. She didn't want to fight with her sister, but this weekend was the only chance either one of them would ever have to go to a bush party—well, at least the only chance until they were really old, like 25 or something—too old to care about a good time, anyway. Their parents would certainly never give them permission to go to one, which is what made this a perfect opportunity—the girls were home alone for the weekend.

"Come on, Bec. It's one night in your life. It'll be fun, you'll see. But you know we should have left by now. We have quite a drive ahead of us."

Rebecca sighed. "Well, I'm certainly not letting you go by yourself."

As Rebecca backed the car out of the driveway Lindsay was all but vibrating with excitement, but 20 minutes later, when they were stuck in traffic and not even close the city limits, her excitement had turned to frustration. "The trip will go faster when we get on the highway," she said, trying to sound positive.

"It'd better," Rebecca replied. "I don't want to be driving around in the dark trying to find some godforsaken spot I've never been to before."

When they eventually did pull onto the highway the traffic was, indeed, moving well, and both sisters relaxed.

Rebecca plugged her MP3 player into the car's connector and cranked up the volume. Nickelback wasn't Lindsay's favourite, but this was one time she wasn't going to complain about having to endure her sister's taste in music.

The two were happily and loudly singing along as they crested a slight rise in the road, when they realized the traffic ahead had stopped. Rebecca slammed the brakes on hard and fast.

"Whew. Good reaction there, Bec. There must have been an accident up ahead. I hope no one is hurt."

"It looks like the back-up goes on forever. There's not much point in just sitting here idling. Look, the cops are cutting off all but one lane. If we can make our way over to the shoulder, I can back up to that last exit. After that I guess we'll have to find our way on back roads."

Lindsay nodded. Her faith in their ability to get to the bush party was wavering, but the whole thing had been her idea so she hated to say anything, especially now that Rebecca seemed determined to make the trip happen. Besides, they were off the highway and heading along a deserted dirt road in no time.

"Okay, Linds, we're making good time now."

A little too good actually, in Lindsay's estimation. "Hey, slow down a bit, would you?" she told her sister, but it was too late. The car had hit a deep rut in the road and began to skid back and forth on the gravel. Terrified, Rebecca managed to keep the car on the road and bring it to a stop.

"Are you all right?" Rebecca asked, grabbing onto Lindsay. She nodded. "You?"

"Yeah, I am, but the car's sure not. We'd better see how bad the damage is."

Lindsay nodded as they got out of the car.

"Well, we're not going to make it to the party, that's certain," Rebecca said, assessing the damage. "Actually, I'd say we're not going anywhere tonight unless we can get some help. The back right tire is ripped to shreds, and it's getting so dark that even if I knew how to change it I wouldn't be able to until morning."

"I'm so sorry. I got us into this. What are we going to do?" Lindsay asked, her voice shaking.

"We passed a house a little way back. It wasn't far from the road. Maybe the people there will let us use their phone," Rebecca suggested.

As the nervous girls approached the frame bungalow they could see lights shining through the windows, but no one answered their knocks. They'd all but given up hope when the door opened.

"Hello, hello," an elderly man greeted them enthusiastically. "The missus said she heard someone at the door, but we don't get many visitors these days so I thought she was imagining things. What brings you to our door this fine summer evening? Is there something we can do to help you?"

"Thank you," Rebecca said. "Yes, there is something. If we could just use your phone, we'd appreciate it. Our car's got a flat."

"Ah," the old man said, rubbing his chin. "I'm sorry to say the phone is a bit of a problem. It hasn't been hooked up again since the fire."

Lindsay couldn't believe what she was hearing. They must have arrived at the only house in the county, maybe in the entire province, without a phone. Could their luck get any worse?

Seeing their concern, the man stepped back from the doorway. "Come in, come in. Don't worry," he added. "You can stay the night here. There's an extra room, and we love having company. We can deal with the car in the morning. Nothing ever seems as bad after a good night's sleep. But in the meantime, come on into the kitchen and meet Martha. My name's Henry, by the way."

Rebecca and Lindsay exchanged glances before introducing themselves to the man and following him into a warmly lit kitchen filled with the aroma of fresh baking.

"We have guests, Martha!" he exclaimed enthusiastically.

"Oh my," the elderly woman responded, patting her white hair and smoothing her gingham apron. "I must look a sight, but at least I can offer you fresh cinnamon buns."

Soon all four were seated around a table in the middle of the kitchen enjoying warm, sweet buns and chatting amiably. Too embarrassed to admit that they'd been heading to a bush party, Lindsay fudged the truth by saying they'd been on their way to visit friends.

"I do love meeting young people," Martha told the couple. "Always so full of life. I could go on chatting like this forever, but it's getting late and you must both be tired. Come and I'll show you to your room."

"Thank you both," Lindsay said. "You've been very kind. Please let us pay you for your trouble."

"Pay us?" Henry retorted loudly. "There's no way we'll let you pay us."

Martha clucked her tongue and shook her head as she leaned toward the sisters as if speaking in confidence. "You keep your money. We're lucky. We really have no need of it these days."

The couple showed the girls to a bedroom upstairs. Despite the unfamiliar surroundings, both Lindsay and Rebecca fell into a deep sleep as soon as they tucked under the homemade quilt and laid their heads on the feather pillows. They slept soundly until just before daybreak.

"You awake?" Rebecca asked.

"Uh huh," Lindsay replied.

"Let's leave as quietly as we can so that we don't disturb Martha and Henry."

The two girls pulled on their jeans and tip-toed through the house. Rebecca was about to open the door when she stopped. "I'd like to leave them some money. What do you think?"

Lindsay nodded and watched as her sister put a $20 bill on the kitchen table. "It could blow off when we open the door," she whispered. "Tuck it under the sugar bowl."

Both girls reached for the dish at the same time and knocked the metal lid onto the table.

"You're so noisy," Rebecca accused. "Honest to goodness, you make enough noise to waken the dead."

"Let's just get out of here. We can argue later," Lindsay replied.

Outside, the cool morning air had an acrid, smoky tang to it. The area was as deserted as it had been the night before. It didn't look as though anyone had even driven past their car.

"It would have been a much longer night if we'd stayed here in the car. Now that it's daylight, I think we can figure out how to change that tire," Lindsay said.

"We're going to have to try," Rebecca agreed.

Lindsay nodded, and before long they had the car up on the jack.

"Okay, we're done. I'm not sure the wheel's tightened as much as it could be, but as long as we drive slowly, I'm sure we'll make it to the next town."

As they rounded a bend in the road, Lindsay spotted a small building with a single gas pump in front.

"I don't think you could really call that a service station, but it might be all we need," Rebecca said as she steered the car to the front of the building.

"Morning, ladies," a tall, thin man said as he wiped his oil-covered hands with an oil-soaked rag. "Is there something I can do for you?"

"If you could check that the right rear wheel is on well enough to get us back to the city, we'd be most appreciative," Lindsay said.

The words were barely out of her mouth before the man was crouched down with a wrench in his hand, giving each bolt an extra bit of pressure.

"That'll get you back to the city no problem," he said. "But don't wait too long before you replace the spare. You just never know when you'll have a flat tire."

"We found that out the hard way last night and ended up spending the night with strangers," Rebecca said.

"Strangers? I have to say I'm a bit shocked. You ladies don't look like you'd be the type to do something that dangerous," the man said quietly.

"Thanks for your concern, and you're right. We wouldn't have normally, but we didn't have a choice. Besides, we were fine. They were the sweetest old couple you ever met in your life," Lindsay assured the man.

"Maybe you know them," Rebecca added. "Martha and Henry? Their house is just back there."

The man stared from Lindsay to Rebecca and back to Lindsay again. The sisters wondered if he was going to say anything more to them or if they should just leave.

When he finally did speak, the man's voice was flat. "You couldn't have," he said. "That house burned to the ground years ago. Martha and Henry must have been asleep when the fire started because they didn't get out of the house."

Lindsay leaned against the car to steady herself. "That isn't possible. We stayed there last night—at their house. We talked to them for more than an hour in the evening. They served us cinnamon buns in their kitchen."

The man shook his head. "I don't think so."

Rebecca jabbed Lindsay and indicated they should get into the car. As they drove away, Lindsay looked back. The image of the man wiping his dirty hands on a dirty rag receded in the rearview mirror.

"That guy creeped me out big time. At least he tightened the lug nuts and didn't charge us anything," she said, sounding relieved. "Bec, let's drive back past that house on our way back out onto the highway."

"We need to get back into the city. We have to replace that tire or Dad will know we wrecked it."

"They won't be home until evening, and this will only take a few minutes. The house is just up over that ridge."

But it wasn't. They stopped the car, got out and looked all around. There was no house anywhere to be seen. All they could find was an overgrown path leading to the blackened foundation of what had once been a small house. The corner of a $20 bill fluttered under a glass bowl with a badly rusted lid.

Finger of Fate

"It's the last night of our camping trip and the first night that it hasn't rained. It'd be a shame to waste it. Let's build a bonfire, roast some marshmallows and tell ghost stories," Sarah suggested.

"Only wet kindling could stand between us and your most-excellent plan," her fiancé Patrick chimed in enthusiastically.

Soon Patrick, Sarah and a half-dozen of Sarah's relatives were gathered around a roaring bonfire with marshmallows precariously impaled on sticks.

"Sarah, you're the one who suggested this. You'd better tell the first story," her 13-year-old cousin Jessica prompted.

After initially protesting that she couldn't talk because her mouth was full of sticky sweetness, the young woman finally relented—but not before warning everyone that her story probably wasn't a true one nor, in the strictest sense, was it an actual ghost story. "But it is a family legend, and seeing as this camping trip is sort of a family reunion then maybe it's not out of place. Besides, I always loved to hear it when I was a kid. It's such a romantic tale."

Sarah's last sentence was met with a chorus of groans from the boys and men in the group. She laughed off their teasing and began to relate the tale.

"We all know that our great grandparents, Evelyn and Willard Dickens, came to Alberta so long ago that it wasn't even a province then. They worked hard and their farm was a success…" Sarah introduced the story so well that her audience soon forgot where they were. Instead of breathing in the smoke from their campfire, they began to smell the sharp tang of an approaching thunderstorm just west of their great grandparents' homestead near Airdrie. Sarah's audience could even imagine the tension in Willard's voice as he called out for Evelyn to help him get the animals into shelter…

* * *

"The storm's big and it's moving fast. We don't have much time," Willard told his wife as they hurried to get the last horse and cow into the barn. "We need to make a run for the house."

They were less than 10 metres from the farmhouse when the first clap of thunder shook the ground and a jagged bolt of lightning sizzled from the sky. Seconds later Evelyn lay motionless on the ground.

"Ev! No!" Willard cried, realizing that she had been struck by lightning. He scooped his beloved wife into his arms and carried her into the house. He laid her limp body down on the sofa and knelt on the floor beside her, not willing to believe what he knew to be true—that the bolt of lightning had stopped Evelyn's heart.

Insane with grief, screaming from the pain of his loss, Willard went out into the yard. As the storm raged at him he dug his wife's grave—not knowing that an escaped convict was hiding at the side of the house, watching his every move. The criminal had broken out of a jail east of there and had made his way this far west by stealing and pillaging. He'd intended to ask Willard and Evelyn for a meal and shelter from the storm. If they'd refused, he'd planned to simply take what he needed, any way he had to.

In the kitchen Willard wiped his wife's face and straightened her clothing. She'd always been so full of life, and now that life was gone. Her motionless body seemed to mock the robust woman she'd been just minutes before.

"I'll wrap you in our quilt and bury you myself," he told his wife's unresponsive body before going to the bedroom and stripping the bedclothes from the mattress. As he turned to leave the room, Willard remembered that just before they set sail for their new life in Canada, his mother had given Evelyn a ring. Jewelry wasn't to Evelyn's taste and certainly wouldn't be much use in the wilderness they were heading to, but his mother had been insistent, and they'd both been surprised and touched by the older woman's generosity.

Willard crouched beside Evelyn's lifeless form and told her, "I'll put that ring on your finger. Mother wanted you to have it."

The pit he'd dug was quickly filling with rainwater. Willard took the quilt outside and laid it in the hole. Then, slowly, he returned to the house, picked up his wife's body and carried it to the freshly dug grave. Gently he laid Evelyn in the ground and tucked the edges of the cover around her. He stood by the grave for a long time, unable to decide whether he was brave enough to kill himself to join his wife or brave enough to continue living without her. In the end he couldn't decide, so he left the grave open and, sobbing, went inside.

The convict had been watching closely, and from the moment he spotted the ring he had no trouble deciding exactly what he was going to do. He jumped into the pit beside Evelyn and tugged at the ring to pull it off, but his hands were so slippery from the rain and the mud that he couldn't get it. The thief knew that he didn't have long. He pulled his knife from its sheath and, with a single practiced arc, cut off

Evelyn's finger. Much to his shock, blood began to pump out of the wound.

Then the woman moved.

The thief was terrified. Screaming, he tried to scramble from the grave, but in the mud and his panic he slipped and fell onto his own knife.

Willard heard the commotion and ran outside. He pulled the man off his wife and, to his great joy, saw that her mouth was twitching. Evelyn was alive! He hoisted her over his shoulder and hurried with her back into the house. He bound her hand as best he could and warmed her body near the fire. By morning the storm had abated and Evelyn was semi-conscious. Willard saddled their fastest horse and rode to a neighbouring farm.

"Get the doctor for me. Fast," he told them. "My Evelyn is in a terrible way. She's nearly dead from a lightning strike. A man's been hurt too."

For the rest of the day Willard stayed by his wife. With every passing hour she gained strength, and by the time the doctor arrived she was sipping broth from a cup.

All the while Willard didn't as much as glance into the grave. He knew that the stranger was dead. He'd ask the doctor to pry Evelyn's amputated finger from the dead man's fist.

* * *

Sarah looked around at the people gathered by the campfire. They'd all been listening intently to her tell the family legend.

"Oh man, that's gross," Jessica squealed, bringing everyone around the campfire back into the present.

Sarah laughed. "I guess in a way it is gross, isn't it? But you know, Jess, if Evelyn had died that day then our grandmother wouldn't have been born, and none of us would be here to appreciate the story. That ring is still in the family."

Sarah's father commented, "You told the story well. But I have something to add to the beginning of the tale. The night before Willard and Evelyn were to sail to Canada, Willard's mother gave that ring to her daughter-in-law with firm instructions that it must always be passed down through the generations. She stressed that without the ring there wouldn't be any future generations."

Once again the audience around the campfire was whisked away to their family's distant past.

* * *

"You must take this ring with you to Canada," Willard's mother insisted.

But Evelyn was clearly uncomfortable with the woman's sudden generosity. Her mother-in-law sighed and pulled Willard's wife closer to her. The story she shared was one Evelyn never forgot.

"My mother gave this ring to me on her deathbed," Willard's mother told Evelyn. "I could see that she was struggling to tell me something as she gave it to me, but there was so little life left in her that she hadn't the strength to make me understand what it was she wanted to say. All she could do was put the ring into my palm. She died a few hours later. That night after her body had been washed and laid out in the parlour, I went to bed. I'd only just fallen asleep when my mother's ghost came to me and warned me that I should never part with that ring until it was time to hand it down to the next generation. She explained that the ring is a talisman. It will keep our family safe. Then her spirit faded from view, leaving an echo, 'Remember my words, remember my words.'"

* * *

For several seconds silence hung in the air around those who had been listening to the story.

Sarah's father cleared his throat before continuing. "As it happens, I brought the ring along with me for our camping weekend because, now that you and Patrick are getting married, the heirloom is yours."

Crying Uncle

"Did you hear that?" Natalie asked her twin brother, William, as the 10-year-olds sat happily on the beach staring out at Pigeon Lake.

"Hear what?"

"I dunno. Maybe nothing, I guess," she answered.

"Hey, wait! Yeah, I do hear something. Someone's calling." William said.

Natalie nodded and put her finger to her lips to shush her brother. "There it is again. Someone *is* calling—for help. It sounds like it's coming from that little island. We'd better go get Mom and Dad."

The pair burst into the cabin, where their father was wiping the winter's grit and dust from the windows and their mother was sweeping the kitchen floor.

"Someone's on the island," Natalie told them excitedly.

"They're calling for help," William interrupted.

"It's true, really. He's in trouble out there," Natalie added.

Tony and Melissa, the twin's parents, exchanged glances. They could tell that the kids were serious in their concern, but they also knew that there was no one else at the lake this early in the season.

"I think you probably just heard the wind blowing through the pine forest," their father suggested.

"Or an animal, perhaps," their mother added.

Now it was the children's turn to exchange glances. They didn't look convinced that their parents' explanations were correct.

William turned to his sister. "You think?" Natalie shrugged her shoulders in reply.

"Mom, when's Uncle Brett coming up?" William asked.

"Later today," Melissa told her son. "Why do you ask?"

"I don't know," the boy mumbled. "Just thought of him, I guess."

"Let's make some hot chocolate. I've just unpacked it," Tony suggested, hoping to distract the children from obsessing over whatever sounds they thought they'd heard.

"We'll move the table so that we can sit facing the lake," Melissa added. The twins knew that this suggestion didn't necessarily mean their mother would be keeping an eye out for the person her children were so sure they'd heard. Their mother was from Prince Edward Island and, although she loved the prairies and Alberta especially, she also loved to be looking out onto water.

"Can we take our drinks out back and wait for Uncle Brett?" Natalie asked.

Tony laughed and nodded. "There's obviously no way we can compete for their attention when my younger brother, the wilderness guide, is in the equation."

The moment William and Natalie saw their uncle's truck pulling into the driveway they ran toward it. "Uncle Brett, Uncle Brett," they called together.

"Please come with us out on the lake," William pleaded excitedly. "Natalie and I were on the beach this morning and we heard someone calling for help. Dad and Mom think it's just other sounds playing tricks on our imaginations, but they didn't hear it for themselves."

"We're worried, Uncle Brett," Natalie added. "We were both positive that it was someone calling for help.

Brett looked toward the lake. "That's a pretty stiff breeze blowing out there right now. If anyone was in trouble this morning I sure hope they've found safety by now—either that or it's going to be too late to help them."

"I don't think anyone's drowned. It sounded as though he was stranded on the island," William explained.

"He? You heard this voice clearly enough to know it was a man's voice?"

"Definitely," William confirmed.

"I heard it first," Natalie added as the trio walked down to the dock. "He was calling for help."

"Okay, I hear you guys, but first let me see what your parents have to say about all of this," Brett told his niece and nephew. "I need to go and say hello to them at least before I do anything else."

Once inside the cabin it didn't take long for the twins' parents to convince Brett that there was no need for concern.

"I brought along an extra-giant-sized jigsaw puzzle. That should take everyone's minds off the strange sounds from the lake," Brett announced.

Tony enthusiastically endorsed the distraction, and Melissa agreed as long as they worked at the table by the window overlooking the lake. Predictably, it didn't take long for Natalie and William to lose interest in fitting the colourful little pieces of cardboard together. They excused themselves from the table and wandered off to play a computer game. Soon they heard a third chair scrape back from the table, and their uncle announced that he was going to the trailer they'd set up as his bedroom to get unpacked.

More than an hour later, Melissa called the twins from their game and suggested that they go out to the trailer and let their uncle know that dinner would be ready shortly. "I'm betting he's fallen asleep out there," she added.

But the trailer was empty. Brett was nowhere to be seen.

"That's all right," their mother said when they told her. "He's probably just gone for a walk. I'm sure he won't be long, and dinner will keep until he's back."

But by 7:00 Brett had still not arrived back at the cabin. The twins and their parents were anxious to eat and were beginning to get a bit worried. It wasn't like him to be inconsiderate.

"I think we'd better go out and look for him," Tony suggested. "Mom and I'll drive along the road toward town. You two stay here in case he comes back by another route. We'll phone you before we start back home."

Their parents had only been gone a few minutes when an uncomfortable thought crossed William's mind. "Wait here," he told his sister as he ran toward the boathouse.

Seconds later the boy was running even faster back toward the cabin where Natalie waited for him on the front porch. "Phone Mom and Dad," William said, gasping for air. "The canoe's gone."

Natalie understood at once what must have happened. Their uncle must have paddled out to see if he could find any sign of the voice that she and her brother were sure they'd heard earlier in the day. The fact that he wasn't back yet suggested that Brett could be in serious trouble. He'd been gone long enough to have paddled the entire lake, which was now a frothy field of whitecaps—water far too choppy for anyone to safely navigate in a canoe.

Within minutes the adults were home. Tony ran for the boathouse and steered the motorboat out into the lake, toward the island. He hadn't gone far when he spotted the overturned canoe. His stomach knotted. Brett must have capsized. Was he too late? Why didn't he think to check the boathouse instead of driving into town? Of all the mistakes he'd made in his life, he knew this was the one for which he'd never be able to forgive himself. Tears blurred his eyes. He'd always been like a second father to Brett—except today, when it had counted most and he'd let him down.

Then, over the sound of the wind, he heard something. Tony cut the engine. Nothing. He shook his head and leaned forward. That was a voice. It had come from the island.

"Over here!"

This time he heard it distinctly, and it wasn't just any voice—it was his brother's voice.

"Over here, Tony! I'm over here—on the island!"

Tony peered through the gathering darkness. There he was. Brett was standing at the shore of the small island. The terror for both men was over.

Neither man spoke until they were safely in the boathouse and the boat's outboard motor had been silenced. Once they were back in the warm, well-lit cabin, Melissa set out big bowls of stew for everyone.

"Sorry to scare all of you like that," Brett said between spoonfuls of steaming beef and vegetables. "I'm sure you know why I went out on the lake. It was bothering me that you kids had heard that voice so clearly, yet we hadn't been able to see anyone. I was worried that we'd left someone in need of help. I should have let you know where I was going."

"And you shouldn't have taken the canoe out when the lake was so rough," Tony reprimanded. "It's odd, though, isn't it, that the kids thought they heard someone calling for help this morning and that you ended up calling for help this evening?"

Melissa took a deep breath. "I think I have an explanation for what happened today. In the Maritimes, supernatural experiences are an accepted part of daily life, and it's well known that children are more receptive to psychic phenomena than adults are. As odd as it may seem, I'm sure that what William and Natalie heard this morning was a harbinger, a forerunner if you will, of Brett's call for help this afternoon."

"Do you mean that somehow we heard something from the future?" William asked.

Melissa nodded.

"But if we hadn't heard that voice in the morning then Uncle Brett wouldn't have gone out on the lake and had that accident," Natalie pointed out. "It's like the whole thing goes in a circle."

"When I was a girl I remember being told that bodies of water like lakes or oceans or even rivers can make our psychic world behave oddly. It could be that out there near the island, the fabric of time is a bit thin."

William looked confused. "So what we heard was a ghost from the future?"

Melissa nodded again.

"I guess we can't expect to understand everything in this world of ours. We're just glad you're home safe with us, Brett," Tony said, sounding relieved and happy that the family's strange experience was finally over.

The Man in the Woods

Jodi and Chris were pleased beyond words when they were finally able to move out of their cramped little apartment in Fort McMurray. They were pleased for themselves, but they were even more pleased for their children.

"Which one of the kids do you think will enjoy the house in the country more—Nathan or Katie?" Jodi asked as she and Chris were getting into bed the night before the big move.

Chris thought for a moment before answering. "I'm inclined to think Nathan might because the wide-open fields and the woods around that house are just perfect for a six-year-old boy to roam about in, but then Katie's a bit older and I think she's even happier to leave all the concrete around here. Hmmm… I guess I'd have to answer your question by saying that I couldn't even guess. We'll have to wait and see."

As it turned out, even several months after the move, Chris still couldn't have told Jodi who was happier in the new place, Katie or Nathan, because both kids simply loved living in the country.

One evening after tucking the children into bed, Jodi watched as Chris stoked the embers in the fireplace. Once the blaze was strong, Chris turned to his wife, smiling. "Living here is great, isn't it? I'm glad we moved. I was worried for a while that we might find this house too isolated after living in the city for so long. After all, there's only us here, not another soul for miles around, but that just hasn't been an issue for any of us, has it?"

"You're right, and haven't the kids blossomed since we've been here? Both of them have grown as strong and agile as can be. They always have such good colour in their cheeks these days," Jodi confirmed before adding, "For what it's worth, we might not be as alone out here as we think we are."

"Huh?" Chris asked absently.

"The kids, every few days they talk about the old man in the woods. They say that they don't see him every day, but they certainly look for him. I don't think they even know his name, but he teaches them about the trees and the plants and animals. They seem to really like him."

Chris laughed. "I love it! They have an imaginary friend, that's all."

Jodi didn't reply. She hoped her husband was right, but she wasn't entirely convinced. Nor was she entirely comfortable with the situation.

Over the next week, Jodi made a point to gently question her children after they'd been playing outside. Both Katie and Nathan were very forthcoming about their new friend. They seemed almost proud to share details about their adventures with him. Anxious to keep the lines of communication open, Jodi put an effort into being as positive as she could, always making comments that were some sort of variation on, "Sounds as though you've found a nice friend." The youngsters always agreed enthusiastically—until the day Katie came home from playing outside for the afternoon clearly feeling out of sorts.

"Sometimes that man in the woods can be a bother," the girl told her mother.

"In what way?" she asked as casually as she could.

"We can't always find him," Katie explained.

"Maybe he's busy somewhere else with other children," Jodi suggested, trying to play along with the children's game.

Nathan joined the conversation, shaking his head emphatically. "It's not like that, Mom. He's always there, but sometimes we can't see him and other times we can barely see him."

"I see," Jodi said, although in fact she didn't see at all. What she did do was make a serious mental note to talk to Chris about this situation.

As soon as the children were in bed that night, Jodi broached the subject of the children's imaginary friend. "Chris, I'm really not comfortable with the kids and this guy in the woods. I think we need to do something about it."

"For goodness' sake Jodi, there is no 'guy in the woods' as you put it. Leave it alone. They're just having fun," Chris said, and disappeared behind the section of the newspaper he'd started to read before supper.

That night the first snow of winter began to fall, and it kept on falling until the world around the family's house in the woods was blanketed in a deep covering of white. The next morning Katie and Nathan were so anxious to get out and play in the fresh snow that they could hardly eat their breakfast.

"I wonder what the man in the woods will think of all this snow," Katie said to her brother between bites of corn flakes.

Before the boy had a chance to ponder his answer, Jodi interjected. "How about you bring your friend home for lunch today. I'd like to meet him."

The children clearly thought that was a terrific idea. They bundled up in their winter clothes and headed outside.

"Don't forget to bring the man in the woods home for lunch with you. I'll make something special," Jodi called out after them.

When noon approached, Jodi set an extra place at the table in order to go along with the pretense of "the man in the woods," but she wasn't surprised a few moments later when she saw only Nathan and Katie trudging up the walk.

"Was this one of the days your friend was hard to see?" she asked.

"Oh no, we saw him," Katie answered, "but he didn't want to come home with us. He said he'd wait until we came back."

"And he said to tell you and Dad not to worry, that he's here for us," Nathan added.

The sincerity in the children's voices sent a shiver up Jodi's back. For the first time, she was really worried about what she hoped was an innocent figment of childish imaginations.

"Let's all stay home this afternoon," Jodi suggested with enthusiasm that sounded artificial even to her own ears. "We can make a fire and roast marshmallows and read stories."

"Yeah, let's!" the brother and sister yelled.

"First though, we'd better let the man in the woods know," Katie added.

Jodi had to laugh at their loyalty to an imaginary entity but decided to go along with them this time because she knew they'd only be gone for a few minutes.

But when the children weren't home half an hour later, her amusement turned to concern. She put on her coat and went outside. She was grateful for the new-fallen snow because the tracks from her children's snow boots were easy to follow—until they suddenly stopped.

In the middle of the east field, about two-thirds of the way to the edge of the woods, the children's footprints simply stopped. It was as if something had plucked her son and her daughter from the earth.

They were never seen again. Indeed, the man in the woods had been there for them.

Ask and It Shall be Given

Ellen sat alone in the big old house in High Level. She rocked back and forth slowly in the chair that had been hers for more than 50 years, since her first child had been a newborn.

"I'm so lonely," she cried, tears running down her cheeks. "If I'd known that I'd be all alone in my old age, I wouldn't have tried so hard to get better from that pneumonia a few years back."

Even though her vision was blurred with tears, a movement in the corner of the room caught the elderly woman's attention. She squinted but still couldn't identify the unfamiliar shape. What was it? She took off her glasses and rubbed her eyes, distracted enough for the moment to forget the misery of her loneliness.

"If I didn't know better, I'd swear there was a person standing in the doorway," she mumbled in confusion.

"Hello, Ellen," a deep, masculine voice said.

"Don't hurt me," the frightened woman pleaded.

"Hurt you? My dear, that's the last thing I'd do. You don't recognize me, do you?"

Ellen shook her head. Terror spread through her body, washing away any traces of the loneliness she had been feeling.

"I'm Harry. We were classmates in high school. I had such a crush on you, and you never even knew I existed."

"Harry? Harry Graham? But you left town right after graduation."

"Oh, so you did know my name," the misty figure sounded surprised. "Yes, that's me. I died this morning, but everyone gets a chance to visit with someone if they want to, and I chose you."

"Am I dying?" Ellen asked.

"No, sadly for me you're not, but you won't be lonely anymore, Ellen. I've decided to spend my afterlife haunting you."

Old and Ugly

There had been a decided swagger in Kaitlyn's step since she'd become a member of her school's in-crowd. It had taken six months of concentrated effort to work her way into the clique, but it had been so worth it. These girls were the ultimate in cool and now, by extension, she was too. She did hate having to give up all the extracurricular music programs she'd been involved in, but you could either be a band nerd or a member of the inner circle—no one could be both. Besides, it wasn't that big a deal. There wasn't even one band trip outside Alberta this year, so at least she wasn't giving up the opportunity to go anywhere new or exciting, whereas just being included with Emily and Laura and the other classy girls made the mere act of going to school a thrill.

This afternoon, for instance, she'd promised her new friends that she'd meet them at their favourite coffee shop on 17th Avenue. No one in the band was nearly sophisticated enough to even know about anything so urban and chic. Everything about the recent change in her life warmed Kaitlyn's smug little heart.

As a matter of fact, her head was so far in the clouds as she hurried toward the café that she didn't see the elderly woman walking toward her until they bumped into one another—hard. Kaitlyn could feel that she'd knocked her off balance and reached out to steady her, but as she did, the youngster remembered her newly elevated status. Neither Emily nor Laura would take kindly to seeing her hanging onto an ugly old crone.

"Watch where you're going, you old witch!" Kaitlyn yelled.

"Ah, my precious," the woman replied, poking a gnarled finger in the girl's face. "You are more right than you know. I am old and wrinkled, but you are weak and shallow. One day you'll be old and wrinkled too. That day will come sooner than you think, missy, you mark my words."

"I'll mark nothing of yours," Kaitlyn replied, hurrying away to the security of her new friends in their coffee shop hangout. She would have liked to have told them about the altercation she'd just had, but at the last minute decided not to. She didn't want anything even remotely negative to come between her and her bright, promising future of popularity.

The next morning Kaitlyn sprang from bed as she had been doing every morning since her acceptance by the campus queens. She ran to the bathroom to wash her face—and screamed at the top of her lungs. The wrinkled, sagging face of a 90-year-old woman stared back at her in the mirror.

Cemetery Walk

Most of the people who knew Rick Turner thought he was weird—even Rick himself occasionally wondered about his strange hobbies. For one thing, he was a big-time *Star Trek* fan. He pretty much structured his life around Trekkie conventions, especially the ones held in the small, southeastern Alberta town of Vulcan, a community that capitalized on the coincidence of sharing a name with the supposed birthplace of the show's popular character Mr. Spock.

But *Star Trek* wasn't all that intrigued Rick. He was fascinated by almost anything paranormal—the possibility that somewhere in the rugged vastness of the Rocky Mountains, at least one Sasquatch family lumbered about hidden from the prying eyes of civilization, that lake monsters existed and that UFOs toured the galaxy. His view of reality hadn't made life easy for him. Over the years he'd taken an awful lot of mean-spirited teasing about his beliefs, and by this point in his life, he only felt accepted and safe from criticism when he was with other self-confessed paranormal geeks.

Unfortunately, empathy didn't run very thick in Rick's veins, and he took advantage of those rare occasions when he did feel comfortable by making cruel fun of anyone who expressed a belief in the one area of the supernatural that he didn't subscribe to—ghosts. He liked to give the impression that only folks who weren't too bright would have any interest in the spirit world. He'd managed to hurt a lot of people's feelings that way, but in his warped assessment, this somehow evened the score with those people who had teased him and somehow justified his own cruelty.

In reality, however, there was an entirely different reason for his mocking. Rick Turner was utterly terrified by the very idea that a disembodied soul could somehow roam the earth. His fear was so great that he didn't even like to hear about ghosts. Sometimes he would even pass up potentially great paranormal conferences just because the topic of ghosts was on the agenda. Other times, though, the temptation to attend, even if ghosts were going to be discussed, was just too great.

And so it was the night his car broke down on a secondary highway just east of Edmonton. He'd had a very full weekend at a paranormal symposium, where he'd traded information with other Trekkies, listened to an expert on cattle mutilation and crop circles, and even spent what he considered to be quality time heckling a speaker who had written a book of true ghost stories.

When his car lurched to a stop, Rick wasn't much concerned. He'd been letting his mind wander so much that he presumed he'd just taken his foot off the accelerator by mistake. Unfortunately, it wasn't that simple. The car had stalled right there in the middle of a narrow secondary highway, and no matter how hard he tried, he couldn't get it started again. He wasn't the least bit keen on the idea of spending the rest of the night in the car; the only alternative seemed to be hoofing it. After walking for close to an hour in the inky darkness, he was overjoyed to see lights glowing in the window of a house off in the distance. Maybe someone there could help him.

Now Rick had learned his high school geometry well, and he knew that the shortest distance between two points was a straight line—and that shortest possible distance was exactly what his tired legs needed. But as it turned out, this particular straight line cut a path directly through a graveyard. The man was, in a word, scared. He was also uncomfortably aware that his options were limited. It was a long way back to his car, and in all the time he'd been walking, not as much as one vehicle had driven by. Tentatively, he stepped off the road toward the cemetery, being very careful to keep his eyes trained on the house in the distance.

"Keep focused," he told himself. "Keep your eyes on the prize, and that prize is the house off in the distance. Ignore the cemetery. Besides, just like you told that stupid speaker this afternoon, there's no such thing as ghosts anyway."

Unfortunately, following his own advice meant that he didn't notice the water-filled culvert between the road and the cemetery fence. By the time he recovered his footing, Rick was not only scared and tired but now also soaking wet.

He climbed the rotting plank fence and lowered himself onto the cemetery grass. With each step he took, his wet sneakers made gurgling sounds that sounded disturbingly like someone was being choked. The trees surrounding him, their branches still bare from winter, seemingly stretched cruelly twisted fingers down at him, pointing him out to the souls trying to rest under his feet. Pine trees at the edge of the graveyard moaned as a sudden gust of wind blew through them.

"I can't do this," he said out loud to himself, tears of fear coursing down his cheeks. "I'm too scared. I don't think I can keep going. I'll have to go back to the car and just wait there until morning. Please don't let me have disturbed any of the souls."

Rick turned around, ready to sprint back to the road—and found himself face-to-face with a middle-aged woman.

He screamed in fright and slammed his right hand against his chest and his left hand over his mouth. "Oh dear God, you scared me," he told the woman, rather unnecessarily. "What on earth are you doing here?"

"Oh, I walk here frequently," she replied with a smile warm enough to make Rick realize with embarrassment that he'd been rude. He probably scared her at least as much as she scared him. He should have explained his own presence there before asking questions of a stranger.

He breathed in what he hoped was a calming breath and told the woman, "My car is broken down and I'm trying to get to that house over there, but I'm scared because I've never walked through a cemetery before."

"I was scared too when I first got here, but by now it just feels like home," the woman answered—before vanishing into a column of mist.

It took a moment for the reality of his surreal situation to register with Rick. When it did, he fainted dead away.

3
Full
Moon

Friday's Treat

There's a certain little community not far from Drumheller where, all in all, life is good, especially if you're partial to predictable. On warm summer days, for instance, you can count on the fact that everyone opens their front doors by 8:30 in the morning, just leaving their screen doors closed to keep the mosquitoes out. And, at least during fair weather days, those doors stay exactly that way until 10:00 at night when, within five minutes of one another, they are closed and locked.

But that certainly isn't all that's comfortingly predictable. Everyone knows they can always count on Fran's Bakery to make the best apple pie this side of heaven, as sure as they know that Bob the hockey rink attendant will always have an unlit stub of a cigar in his mouth.

One routine peculiar to this particular town was one created by old Mrs. Griffiths. Every Friday, without fail, she would leave her cookie tin out on her front step, just in time for the kids coming home from school. All the townsfolk agreed that it was an odd habit Mrs. Griffiths had. Yes, they supposed it was thoughtful and kind, but odd all the same. Her house was set off by itself so no one ever saw her set the cookie tin out on her porch, but even so, Fridays by 3:30, there it was, and had been for years—but only on Fridays.

Stranger still, there weren't any cookies in the tin. Instead there were dimes. For at least three generations, youngsters had been picking up a dime each every Friday. No one gave a thought to how the routine had started, but they all knew about it just as they all knew that they were only welcome to take one dime, and for the most part, that's what they did.

Back a few years ago when a dime was worth something, most boys and girls went directly from Mrs. Griffiths' front porch to the candy store. But when a dime would no longer buy anything, the Friday routine became little more than a rite of passage because, of course, the very little children were too young to stray so far from their route home and the older kids saw the stop as being decidedly uncool.

Sometimes the moms in town would scold their sons and daughters to remember their manners and to knock on Mrs. Griffiths' door and tell her thanks for the treat. Some kids tried that a few times, but they always reported back to their mothers that Mrs. Griffiths didn't seem pleased at all to be called to the door. No matter how polite they'd been, she just told them in an angry-sounding voice to take their dime and be gone. Besides, they told their moms, the old lady's face always looked blurry through the screen door, and for some reason the children found that a bit unnerving.

Jim English and Bill Nelson had lived in the area all their lives. As youngsters in early elementary school, they'd looked forward to being old enough to visit Mrs. Griffiths' porch on Fridays. Then by junior high, they considered themselves quite mature and worldly and were suitably disdainful of the childish tradition. After all, what good was a dime? By now they were really mature. They'd graduated from high school several years before and were even too old to hang out on Main Street. They still hung out together, but just on weekends and usually while they worked at restoring Bill's vintage Mustang.

One Saturday morning as the two young men lovingly buffed the second coat of primer on the car's rear deck, they got to reminiscing.

"Remember the prank we played on Mr. Hubbard, the gym teacher?" Bill asked.

Jim chuckled before saying, "I do. Man, the look on his face was really something, wasn't it?"

"Those were good times. I wonder if the kids today have as much fun."

Jim flicked an errant bug off the car's freshly polished surface and then gazed off into space. "I've never told anyone this, but the one thing I always hated doing was going to Mrs. Griffiths' house on Fridays when she put out that stupid cookie tin full of dimes. Once a week for three years—grades four, five and six, if I remember correctly. Believe it or not, I started to dread the thought of that routine even toward the end of grade three. I was so glad to get to junior high and supposedly be too grown-up for it."

"You're weird, man," Bill informed his friend. "That was fun. Those dimes were the last easy money in my life."

"Oh yeah, right, you're so hard done by. But seriously, hasn't it ever occurred to you that the whole set-up with old lady Griffiths was a bit freaky?" Jim probed, warming to his subject.

"Freaky? No, it was tradition. Still is from what I hear. Honestly, I think it's one of the things that binds the people of this town together. It runs right through the generations. Ask your parents. I know mine remember getting their weekly dime. My father says that dime would buy him enough candy to give him an upset stomach."

Jim jumped in. "That's what I mean, bozo! Think about it. Your parents were kids more than 40 years ago, and Mrs. Griffiths was an old lady even then. How can someone who was old 40 years ago still be alive?"

Bill reached around to the fence behind him where a couple of cans of cola stood on the railing. He pulled open the little metal tab, took a swig of the pop, belched and then said, "That's just a perception thing, man. The kids who went to Mrs. Griffiths' yesterday would look at us and think we're old."

Jim shook his head. It was clear he didn't even come close to agreeing.

Bill continued. "Okay, I'll prove it to you. As soon as we're done here today, you and I'll drive out to Mrs. Griffiths' place. We'll go up to the door, introduce ourselves and tell her that we just wanted to thank her for her generosity to everyone over the years. That way we'll both get a good look at her. I'll bet she's not much more than 60 years old."

"I'll drive out there with you, but I'm waiting in the car." Jim's voice was full of conviction. Bill knew there was no way of arguing with him when he sounded like that.

The sun was still high in the sky as they drove to the dead-end street at the edge of town. Neither young man said much during the drive. Bill hummed along to songs on the radio, and Jim seemed to be lost in his own thoughts.

When they reached the odd little house that they'd traipsed to so regularly as kids, Bill thrust the car into park. "I've never seen this place except on Fridays. It looks different without the cookie tin on the porch and all the kids making their way up the steps and back down again," Bill commented.

Jim didn't reply.

"Are you with me on this?" Bill inquired impatiently.

"No. I'm not. I'm not going anywhere near that place," Jim said. "You're right, though, it looks even creepier today than it did on all those Fridays. Just wait a minute before you go. I had a thought on the way out here, but it flitted through my mind so fast I didn't have time to say anything to you. It feels like it had to do with Mrs. Griffiths."

"Well, what is it?"

"Sorry, I can't remember. It felt a bit like a piece of a dream, you know? I can't quite think what it was."

Bill was standing beside the car by now, tapping his foot.

Jim shrugged. "Never mind. Go ahead. Do whatever it is you want to do to prove to me that I was a chicken as a kid, and if I think of what's bugging me, I'll tell you when you get back to the car."

With that, Bill slammed the car door and made his way to Mrs. Griffiths' gate and up the walk. Jim turned away. Maybe he was just a chicken about this place and always had been, but even now he couldn't as much as bear to watch his friend approach the house. Every grinding bit of discomfort he'd felt as a kid, walking along that same path, snaked up his back and into the pit of his stomach.

Jim could hear his friend knocking on the door. *Hurry up Bill,* he silently urged. *Forget it; the old bag's obviously not going to answer the door, and I don't have all day, you know. I'm supposed to run a couple of errands for my grandparents this afternoon.*

"Wait!" he said out loud in the empty car. "That's what I was trying to remember! My grandparents! Even *they* talk about going to Mrs. Griffiths for dimes. I was right all along. There is something wrong with that situation—really wrong."

Jim rolled down the passenger's side window and yelled for Bill to get back into the car, but his friend just gave him a dismissive wave.

Pushing past fear that threatened to paralyze him, Jim knew he had to do something. His childish intuition had been right, and his friend could be in serious danger. Summoning every ounce of courage he could find, he opened the car door and stood on the sidewalk. That was as far as he got before Bill, screaming and waving his arms, fled from Mrs. Griffiths' front porch. He leaped over the small picket fence and kept on running, screaming all the way, oblivious to his friend's effort to stop him.

Jim finally found Bill shaking uncontrollably and huddled into a ball at the back of Luke's Hardware Store between the dumpster and the wall. He was talking gibberish—something incomprehensible about Mrs. Griffiths being transparent, that he'd been able to see right through her.

Jim sat holding his friend until Ryan Davidson, Luke's stock boy, poked his head out the back door of the store to see what the commotion was about. He called the ambulance. The medics sedated Bill for the trip to the hospital. He wouldn't have let them take him otherwise. No matter how they reassured him that he'd be safe, he was terrified they'd make him go back to Mrs. Griffiths' house.

That night the old woman's house burned to the ground. All that was left were ashes. No one knew what caused the fire, but, truth be told, no one put much effort into finding out either. Her house was gone and so, apparently, was she.

Jim still goes to see Bill pretty regularly. His visits have become one of the threads that make up the predictable patterns of the town's fabric. Of course, most of the time Bill is too drugged to even realize he has a visitor; there are times when the staff has to dope him up extra heavily. No one can figure out why, but often on Friday afternoons he still gets extremely agitated.

The Accident

Metal smashed against metal with such ferocity that when what had been a four-door sedan came to rest on the sidewalk, it had been reduced to a mangled metallic jumble. All was still and completely quiet for a moment.

Seconds later, Sue opened her eyes. "You all right, Pete?" her voice cracked oddly as she spoke.

"Think so," the young man replied as he pulled himself up awkwardly from under the dashboard in front of the passenger's seat, where the impact had hurled him. "You?"

"Nothing hurts, so I don't think anything's broken. What hit us?" she asked.

Pete looked out the shattered windshield before answering. "It must have been that transport truck. Not much worry that he'll be okay."

"Can you get your door open? We need to get out of here. I smell gas."

Pete jammed his shoulder against the car door. It creaked and moaned in its twisted resistance but finally gave way. He climbed awkwardly out onto the sidewalk before leaning back in to help guide his girlfriend through the maze of twisted metal and broken glass that used to be a car. "Watch out for all the broken pieces; they're sharp."

Once the young woman was standing on the sidewalk beside her boyfriend, she began to brush them both off.

"Never mind that now," Pete told her. "We need to get away from the car. It's really leaking gas badly."

Taking shelter beside a nearby building, the two watched and listened in horror as the car exploded into a fiery ball.

"We'll need a new car," Sue commented unnecessarily.

"That *so* doesn't matter," Pete assured her, putting his arm around her shoulder. "Neither of us is hurt, which is nearly unbelievable. That truck hit us with a helluva lot of force."

"The driver's on his cell phone, so he's all right. He saw me so he knows we're out of the car. We made eye contact as I walked in front of the truck."

Off in the distance the couple could hear the wail of sirens.

"The trucker must have been calling for help when you saw him on the phone," said Pete.

Pete and Sue tucked themselves into the doorway of the building. Moments later they watched as half a dozen fire-fighters blanketed the flaming car with foam. Ambulances and police cars, sirens screaming, slammed to a stop at the accident scene. Once the inferno that had been their car was smothered in fire retardant, the couple made their way toward the curb. "We need to let them all know that we're okay," Pete said pointing to the wreck.

Sue nodded.

By the time the couple approached the crowd at the curb, the emergency workers were in a heated discussion. One or two of the men occasionally turned toward the man Sue had seen on the phone in the cab of the truck. The young couple waited patiently for a break in the conversation.

"Just before the car caught fire I saw two columns of mist come from the car. It didn't look like smoke, but maybe it was," the trucker explained before adding, "I don't know what could've caused the crash."

The trucker's words snapped Pete's patience completely. "Like hell you don't!" he shouted at the man. If you don't know what caused it, then I certainly do. You were driving on the wrong side of the road as you came up over that hill, idiot. What's the matter with you? Did you think I wouldn't be here to counter the bull you're slinging?"

The trucker ignored Pete's outburst. "I think there were two people in the car, although I could be wrong. Nothing moved in there after the impact, and then just a few seconds later, the thing blew."

A draft of icy air swirled around the group.

"That cold just goes right through a person," one of the medics said quietly.

Sue leaned closer to Pete and whispered, "I don't believe how much that truck driver's lying."

"And how rude! He didn't even acknowledge that I'd spoken," Pete said. "Once the cops take all the measurements that they do, they'll see what happened. I'm betting the trucker fell asleep and his rig drifted over into our lane."

"Just at the wrong time, too," Sue added.

Pete nodded.

"Come here," Sue urged. "You can see better from here. It's really clear from up higher like this. His truck's way over in our lane."

Pete nodded. "Funny that we didn't notice it from this angle before. He's in the wrong. It's totally obvious now that we're up above the wreck."

"We are, aren't we—above the wreck, I mean?" Sue asked. "We're floating. We're looking down at the car. It's amazing; the firefighters must have put out the blaze before the car burned completely. Did you leave your coat on the floor, Pete? It looks like you did. There's a mound of clothes there, anyway."

"We're so far up that I can't see inside the car anymore."

"Oh well, it doesn't matter. It'll be ruined by now for sure, but you can always buy a new coat, if that's what it is lying there. Like you said, the important thing is that neither of us was hurt."

"It's amazing that we weren't, isn't it?" Pete confirmed from their vantage point several hundred metres in the air as the two ambulances slowly and quietly left the accident site.

By the time the firefighters were sure the badly burned car wasn't going to re-ignite, the police had finished documenting the crash scene and the trucks from the coroner's department had arrived, both Sue and Pete were blissfully ensconced in their afterlives. For them, mundane events like a double fatality car accident were already long forgotten.

Honeymoon Hell

In the 1950s, honeymoons weren't nearly the elaborate events that they are now. As a matter of fact, after Ben and Irma were married, some people thought their plan to drive from Drayton Valley to Coronation was extravagant.

Well, maybe it is extravagant, Ben thought, but Coronation was where his favourite aunt and uncle lived. He understood that they were elderly and couldn't make it to the wedding, but he knew they'd love Irma almost as much as he did and he very much wanted to have them meet her.

And so it was that the newlyweds began their journey the day after their wedding, but they only managed to cover 150 kilometres before they were both ready to look for a place to spend the night. When Irma spotted a row of little cabins behind a hand-lettered sign with the word "vacancy" written on it, they decided to pull in.

"It looks like a five-year-old kid made that sign," Ben commented as he steered the truck onto the gravel driveway. "You wait here. I'll go check us in."

A few minutes later he was back to the truck for Irma. "It's our lucky day. They only have one cabin left to rent for tonight," he told his bride as he lifted their suitcase from the bed of the truck.

"Really?" she questioned. "The whole place looks deserted to me."

Ben looked around and realized that Irma was right. There really didn't seem to be anyone else staying there. *I wonder why the guy told me they were so booked up*, he thought as he set down the suitcase in front of the third cabin to the left of the office. There were no numbers on either the door or the key, but the innkeeper's instructions had been clear, so Ben wasn't surprised when he turned the key in the lock and the door to the darkened cabin swung open.

As they fumbled to find the light switch, a strange odour wafted around them. Ben shot a quizzical glance at Irma, who told him that it was likely just the smell of some unusual cleaning product that the housekeeping staff used. They closed the door to the room and the stench grew worse. It wasn't just an unpleasant smell, but oddly it seemed to bring heat with it, stifling heat, the kind that nearly takes your breath away.

Irma opened the window. Ben took off his shirt.

"Something's wrong in here," Irma commented. "Only wickedness could bring this kind of sour heat."

Ben's only response was a mirthless laugh that he hoped didn't reveal his concern.

"Don't you think we should leave?" she asked her husband, who, by this time, was lying on the bed with his hands under his head.

"If we did I'm sure we'd have to drive for miles before we could find another place to stay," Ben answered in a tired-sounding voice. Moments later he was fast asleep where he lay.

Irma perched herself on the edge of a straight-backed chair, the only other piece of furniture in the room. Tears streamed down her cheeks as she stared into the inky black-ness that surrounded her. She had never felt so terrified in her entire life. *If only it wasn't so dark,* she wished between silent sobs, forgetting that sometimes you can be sorry to have a wish come true.

Soon her eyes adjusted to the lack of light, and when they did she saw, off in the corner, a swirling mass of putrid black energy. The evil vortex was oozing ominous dread. At its centre was a pair of red eyes.

This was enough. Irma shook Ben's shoulder until he woke up. "We need to get out of here. Now."

The young man's eyes flew open. He bolted upright.

"This place is haunted," she told him.

They grabbed their luggage and ran from the room to the safety of their truck. Only when they had the doors to the truck locked did either of them speak again.

"It was straight-out wickedness in there," Irma said.

Ben stared mutely into the night and shook his head.

"You don't agree?" she prompted. "Really, Ben, if that wasn't pure evil then what would you call it?" she prompted.

"I wouldn't," he said slowly, his voice shaking. "I wouldn't call it anything for fear it would answer."

A Nudge in the Right Direction

"Any idea why Marv wanted to see us?" Sam paced nervously as he and Milly waited outside the boss's office.

"None whatsoever, although I suspect that if you'd been able to hike up your maturity level, this might not be happening." Milly did nothing to disguise the disdain in her voice.

Sam sighed, trying to relax, but when Big Marvin Stark threw open his office door, both underlings jumped.

"Come in, you two." The words weren't an invitation. They were an order. "No point in mincing words here. You two botched that last assignment pretty badly."

Sam and Milly pointed fingers of blame at one another, but their boss waved off their attempts at evading responsibility.

"I need your word—both of you—that you won't botch this one. If you do, there are a couple of demotions with your names written all over them."

The chastised pair nodded. They'd only worked their way up from stray dog detail a few months ago. That was not a place they wished to re-visit even temporarily, and they understood all too well that once there was a second demotion on record, they'd be an eternity working it off.

"There are a couple of young people I'm extremely interested in encouraging. They're both a bit inept, but we absolutely can't risk having them misplay their parts. Apparently the logistics are complicated, but the word on this one has come straight down from the top. Management as much as told me that the fall-out from a miscue could be horrendous—something about implications for the next generation."

Milly sucked in her breath. *Thanks for the pressure, big boy. Couldn't you have assigned this to someone with a proven track record?*

"Here are their cards," Marvin continued. "The first stage of this exercise has to be operational today, so you'd both better get out of here and onto this right away."

"But, but," Sam sputtered as he and Milly found themselves back out in the corridor.

"Let's read these stats over carefully," Milly suggested, staring at the index cards in their hands.

"I'm nervous, Mill. We can't goof up on this one."

"We'll get it right, Sam. Trust me," she assured him, just before vanishing into thin air.

* * *

By the time the bus pulled away from the curb, Rob was so lost in thought that it took him a while to realize there was someone standing next to the empty aisle seat beside him. Worse, that person was speaking to him.

"Sorry," he muttered as he looked up to see a middle-aged woman staring down at him. "Were you talking to me? I didn't hear you."

"I asked if the seat beside you was taken. If it's not, I'd like to rest my weary bones upon it," the stranger told him.

Rob looked around helplessly. There were plenty of empty seats in the bus. *Why does she want to come and sit beside me?* he wondered, and motioned for her to sit beside him. As he did, Rob noticed that the woman didn't have a coat, or even a jacket or sweater on, just a light cotton uniform with the name "Milly" embroidered on the left side of the blouse. *You can sit here*, Rob thought, *but please don't try to start a conversation with me.*

"Are you a student?" the woman asked.

"Uh-hum," Rob assented, thinking absently that it was getting colder in the bus.

"Been able to avoid student loans so far?" the woman inquired.

Yeah, right, like my finances are any of your business. "Uh-hum," he repeated.

"Well, that shows industry. You have a part time job then?"

"Uh-hum," he repeated.

"And where's that?" the woman asked, pointedly turning her head so that she was literally in Rob's face.

"At the Lethbridge Market," the increasingly annoyed young man replied.

"I bet there are lots of pretty young girls there!" the woman exclaimed.

No, actually, there are more old busy-bodies like you, Rob thought, but said nothing. He turned to stare out the window. *Silly old bag, why'd she have to pick on me?* he moaned to himself.

Just then the bus came to a sudden stop, jolting everyone forward.

"Sorry, folks," the driver called out. "Some woman just ran out in front of the bus. I had to brake hard to miss her. Is everyone all right back there?"

A weak chorus, which included Rob's voice, affirmed that everyone *was* all right. Everyone, that is, except for the woman who had been sitting next to Rob. She was no longer there. She was simply gone.

Weird, he thought, *but as long as she's not pestering me with any more questions, I don't really care where she went or how. Besides, she clearly didn't notice that I'm hardly a social animal.*

The old busy-body had been right, though. There were lots of pretty girls working at the store, but none of them had ever shown any interest in Rob. That was simply a fact of life—one that always put him in a bad mood. *I'll likely never get to date a pretty girl,* he thought glumly as he pulled on the cord to signal the bus driver that he needed to get off at the next stop.

For the first few seconds after Rob walked into the grocery store to begin his shift, his eyes and ears felt suddenly under assault. The place was crowded. People were everywhere: there were line-ups at the check-out stands, people milling in the aisles, bag boys scurrying to get customers' parcels out to their cars and then back into the store where they were already needed once again. The sound system blared a request for a price check at till five before resuming the horrible music that head office insisted the store play every minute it was open.

"Gallagher!" Rob's boss called to him. "Get into the back. A shipment's come in. The truck's here after the delivery hours, but it's produce so it has to be off-loaded quickly. When you're done you can get to work fronting the canned goods aisle; then see what needs topping up over in dairy."

"Uh-hum."

Rob walked toward the loading dock. He threw his coat on a hook and then immediately wished he hadn't. It was darn cold back here. They must have turned the heat down. He looked over to the ramp. There was a truck backed in, but not the usual kind of big rig. This was just a pickup truck with less than half a dozen boxes in it. Three of them had been stacked on the lowered tailgate. *What the heck is going on?* Rob wondered.

"Hi there," boomed the truck driver's voice as he literally jumped out of the cab of his vehicle and onto the loading dock ramp. "I'm Sam," he continued unnecessarily, considering that the name was embroidered on his shirt pocket. "These boxes just need to be stashed around that corner, and then I'll be on my way."

"Uh-hum," Rob replied, as much out of confusion as habit. He grabbed the three boxes from the gate of the truck.

"They need to go over there," Sam said, pointing around the corner of one wall of the loading bay. Before Rob could answer, the man had flipped up the tailgate on his truck and was driving away.

Rob carried the three cartons to the area the man had indicated. As he was setting them down, he heard a small rustling noise. *Mice?* He wondered briefly, but then, out of the corner of his eye, Rob saw something move—a young woman, about his own age, dressed in a store uniform, was standing in front of him. Her presence there surprised him so much that he said, more loudly than he intended, "What are you doing back here?"

The slim girl dropped her head a bit. "Hi, my name is Joan. Today is my first day of work here. I was doing all right out there, but then the crowds and all the noise kind of got to me and I just had to be alone back here in the quiet for a moment. You won't tell anyone, will you?"

Rob shook his head. "No, of course not. I know exactly what you mean. I've worked part time here for years, but I still need to escape back here for a few minutes at a time almost every shift."

"Really?" Joan asked, offering Rob a shy smile.

"Oh, yeah," Rob confirmed. "Now that you've had your few moments by yourself, I guarantee you'll be fine for the rest of your shift. How much longer do you have to work?"

"I'm scheduled until 11:00 tonight, but the head cashier told me that if they didn't need me, she'd send me home earlier. That has me a bit worried because I couldn't give my father a definite time to pick me up," Joan replied quietly.

"Well, on a night as busy as this one, I'd say you have no hope of getting out of here early. I'm through at 11:00, too." Rob hesitated only a moment, his conversation with Milly on the bus earlier flashing through his mind, before surprising himself by saying, "If you don't want to disturb your father that late at night, I could walk you home."

"Thanks, Rob, that would be one less thing on my mind. I can call home on my break and let them know."

Rob grinned broadly at his new-found friend. "Okay, let's get out of here and back on the floor before we both get in trouble for goofing off," he said.

"Thanks again," Joan said as they made their way through the swinging doors and out into the main part of the store. The same noise and bustle they'd both been so glad to escape from only minutes earlier now seemed tolerable.

The evening hours flew past for both Joan and Rob. They saw each other only twice during the balance of their shifts but managed to exchange smiles.

* * *

Neither Sam nor Milly was nearly that busy, though they were both still in the store. Their "shifts," if you could call them that, were over.

"That was a fun one, Milly," Sam confirmed as they watched, invisible to all but each other, from the rafters of the old grocery store.

Milly nodded. "I don't know why Marvin implied that this assignment was going to be so complex. Who knows with him sometimes? Anyway, we did it and now it's time for us to go. I can feel myself fading; can you?"

Sam's vanishing form nodded in agreement. "Until next time then," he called, but Milly didn't hear him, for she had already disappeared.

* * *

Later that evening, Rob and Joan chatted for the entire walk to Joan's front door. During the conversation, Joan admitted that she really was a very shy person and pretty much a homebody when she wasn't working at the store. Rob said that he knew exactly how she felt because he too was shy, and that when he wasn't at work or at the university, he usually had his nose in a textbook at home. Both laughed at the realization that if they hadn't happened to meet face-to-face in that isolated corner of the storeroom, they might never have managed to introduce themselves to one another.

Just before Joan walked into the house and Rob turned to leave, he paused, cleared his throat and, sounding considerably more confident than he felt, said, "There's a movie on at the Rialto that I've been meaning to see. Would you like to go too?"

"Thanks, that would be fun. Give me a call tomorrow. My parents' phone number is in the book," Joan replied with a broader smile than he'd ever seen decorating her pretty face.

* * *

Joan and Rob's friendship blossomed. They saw each other almost daily for the next three years. Their fondness and respect for one another brought out aspects in the other's personality that hadn't been apparent before. Over time, each was drawn out of their shyness. Both became more outgoing, not only with each other but also with other people they met. Their self-confidence and happiness grew in leaps and bounds. Their friendship had made life exciting for both of them.

That friendship remained a bedrock foundation for their lives, even as those lives grew and developed in different directions. Rob graduated with honours and found a job he enjoyed. Joan stayed with the grocery store, but because of the night-school courses Rob encouraged her to take, she became the store's accountant. Five years after they met, Rob and Joan decided to get married. And so they did; Rob married Erin, Joan's sister. Joan married Kyle, the store's credit manager. The two couples live across the street from one another and are all the best of friends.

* * *

Milly and Sam, the ghostly matchmakers, were delighted by the turn of events. Their only purpose had been to inject happiness into the lives of two lonely, shy, young people by giving them a little nudge in the right direction. They hadn't realized their good intentions would take on a life of their own and extend beyond the system of the original couple.

Periodically, Milly and Sam drop in to visit the two happy couples. They always know it's time to leave when one of the four living people makes some comment about the room getting chilly.

Party to Death

Jill Burke had never been so anxious to have Christmas come—and to have it go—because on December 28, she was hosting a party that she hoped would set a new standard for the elegant Calgary neighbourhood of Mount Royal.

She'd scheduled the event with great care. Leading up to Christmas people would be involved with any number of potentially conflicting social obligations, and of course on New Year's Eve and New Year's Day most of the people she wanted to have on her guest list would have other commitments. She just couldn't risk having anyone respond to her engraved invitation with regrets because she had a surprise, something that she wanted to show off to everyone.

When she bought the Mount Royal mansion the year before, Jill finally considered herself equal to the folks she had spent a lifetime envying. This year, however, she figured she had put herself well out in front: she had hired a butler. *No one* else in the neighbourhood had a butler. Lots of households had live-in maids—she had one herself—but no one, absolutely no one else, had a full-time, live-in butler.

And this man was no ordinary butler—if there even was such a thing as an "ordinary" butler. When Jill had hired the man he'd told her that he had an amazing array of unique abilities, and that had certainly proven to be so.

He definitely had a way of polishing her silver tea service that left it shining as it never had before. He'd taught the maid some tricks with food presentation that were absolutely delectable. His most intriguing attribute, though, was his extraordinary thoughtfulness. He seemed to consider each situation carefully and always had at least one helpful comment or suggestion for her. At first it was just inconsequential matters such as recommending that she take an umbrella even on a lovely, sunny day. Inevitably, by the time she was getting ready to head home those days, it was raining. She'd have ruined many an expensive outfit if she hadn't followed his advice. Jill always intended to ask him what radio station he listened to for weather forecasts because his sources were certainly much more accurate than hers.

Another time, as he was seeing her off to work in the morning, he suggested that she slip her court shoes into her gym bag. She loved to play squash during her lunch break but knew her regular partner would be working from home that day, so Jill had planned to go jogging instead. Just before noon, the company's very handsome and eligible new CEO popped his head into her office and asked if he could interest her in a match on the squash court.

And then there was the time that he recommended she leave her car at home and take the train to the office. Jill hated public transit and he knew it. Fortunately, by this time, she was intrigued enough with the butler's advice that she was at least willing to compromise. She drove her car to the park-and-ride, boarded a train and was downtown in just a few minutes. As it turned out, she was the only board member there for the shareholders' meeting. All the others were held up in a traffic jam that had been caused by a car accident. Her boss had been so appreciative that he'd made an official note on her personnel file. For a woman wanting to be on the fast track to a successful career, such notes were monumentally important.

Even so, she'd been surprised when, just a few hours before her big party was due to begin, he told her that he was a gifted palm reader.

"You must do readings for my friends when they're here this evening," she told him. "It'll be such a novelty. They'll love it."

Ever courteous and deferential, the butler bowed his head slightly and nodded.

For several hours after the guests arrived, Jill could see that her new employee was too busy to be interrupted with a request to perform a party game, so she waited until nearly 10:00 before announcing that she had a little entertainment planned.

"My butler is skilled in the art of palm reading, and he's generously agreed to share his talents with us this evening," she explained. "I hope you're prepared to be entertained. I know I am."

Looking rather uncomfortable, the butler acknowledged his introduction. Several people stepped forward immediately and extended their hands for the fun of having their palms read.

The butler told the first guest that he'd soon be making a large charitable donation.

"Not much palm-reading skill needed there," someone called out. "Everyone knows Ian is generous."

Next in line was a woman whom he told to expect a visit from her parents.

"I think he might be right," she told the others.

The partiers were clearly getting caught up in the fun. A man thrust out his palm toward the butler.

"You have a lottery win in your future," he told the man, who simply scoffed, knowing that he never bought lottery tickets. But he didn't see the expression on his wife's face as she reacted to the news.

"Pick me next," a woman called, and made her way to the butler's side with her hand outstretched. After staring intently at her palm for a few seconds, he whispered in her ear.

The woman pulled away as though she'd been touched with something hot. "How could you possibly know that?" she asked in a snarl.

Awkwardness froze the air until the man who'd been standing next to Jill presented his palm for the butler's inspection.

"Hello there," he said to Jill's pride-and-joy butler. "My name's Webster, Theo Webster, and there's no need to whisper *my* fortune when you read it. I have no secrets."

The butler stared at the man's palm, then shifted uncomfortably from one foot to the other.

"Well?" the man prompted.

Jill's new employee stammered. Colour drained from his face. When he finally spoke, there was an edge of nervousness in his voice. "Sir, I ask that you please be very careful as you head home this evening. If you're not, your tiny son could suffer a great tragedy."

"Oh really?" Theo Webster laughed. "That's a good one, because I don't have a son! My wife Michelle is here with me this evening, and she'll vouch for the fact that we're only now talking about getting pregnant."

"Perhaps I'm mistaken, sir," the butler replied before turning to Jill. "With your permission, madam, I should really get back to my regular duties now."

Jill nodded, confused and a bit disappointed at how badly her surprise had come across. Rather than making more fun for her guests, the ploy temporarily silenced them. Fortunately, Theo Webster (*Always such a gracious guest*, Jill thought) broke the awkward hush.

"Let's not worry about this hocus-pocus. Everyone knows I'm fine and will be for many years to come. Let's get on with enjoying Jill's hospitality and each other's company, shall we? It's time to refresh our drinks, I think," he boomed out, a bit too jovially.

Despite the Theo's assertions, the "hocus-pocus," as he put it, evidently *did* worry him because by the time he left the party that night, he'd had considerably more to drink than usual. Worse, he insisted on driving the few blocks home. Not wanting to make a scene in front of her friends and neighbours, Michelle Webster went with him, figuring that not much could happen to them between Jill's front door and their own.

She was very, very wrong. By the time an early morning commuter found their overturned car in the ditch, they were both dead. It wasn't until after the funeral when relatives were clearing out the Websters' house that anyone found the congratulations card that Michelle had tucked under Theo's pillow just before they'd left for Jill's party.

She'd written just two words on it: "We're pregnant!"

Winter Driving

Dawson drove into the snow-covered parking lot feeling relieved and resigned at the same time. It had been a hair-raising drive from Bonnyville; it was a route he'd driven dozens of times and often in winter, but a particularly nasty blizzard had made this trip the worst one ever.

He'd planned this stop in St. Paul anyway to fill up the car with gas, but now he wondered if he shouldn't just spend the night in the old motel out behind the gas bar and coffee shop. By morning the road crews might have had a chance to clear the highway, and besides, driving in daylight was always way easier.

His sneakers crunching in the deepening snow, Dawson made his way across the parking lot to the warmth and companionship of the small, all-night restaurant. Even that short distance made the young man realize how inadequately dressed he was. He cursed himself. It had been a clear, warm for late autumn day when he'd left Edmonton the week before, and though, like any true Albertan, he knew better than to trust the weather, it hadn't crossed his mind to put his pack of emergency winter gear in the trunk.

It sure is crossing my mind now, he thought wryly. *Worse, I'd be the first one to call someone a fool for driving in this weather, as totally unprepared as I am.*

"Hurry up and get in here, young fella," the waitress called out from inside the restaurant. "Close that door behind you quick and give it a good hard tug. The wind is so bad it's been catching and blowing it open every so often. That's the last thing we need is to have the door ripped off."

Dawson nodded and pulled the plate glass door tightly closed before trying to stomp the snow off his shoes on the soggy mat laid out for that purpose. He looked around for a place to sit down. The tables scattered about the room were all occupied by truckers hunched over steaming mugs of strong coffee, so he gave one of the stools at the counter a twirl before sitting down on it.

"Just coffee?" the woman asked, giving the counter in front of him a cursory and unnecessary wipe.

"I think I'd better have a sandwich too if you have one ready."

"Ham and cheese all right? It's all we have left."

Dawson nodded absently, his mind already on the decision he knew he had to make quickly. He cleared his throat and called out to no one in particular, "Excuse me. Does anyone know what the roads are like to the south?"

A few of the men grunted ambiguously. Others said nothing before resuming whatever conversation Dawson's question had interrupted.

Seeing that her customer wasn't getting the information he needed considering the storm howling outside, the waitress turned from the grill she'd been scraping. "A trucker who stopped in on his way northbound told me that south of Smoky Lake the roads were good, but between here and there he said they were treacherous."

Dawson mumbled his thanks, still not sure what to do. He badly needed to be back at work in Fort Saskatchewan the next morning. He'd messed up way too many times as far as his boss was concerned. If his job wasn't on the line already then it was really close, and not showing up could easily clinch the deal. Still, without proper gear and a cell phone, even hitting a patch of ice and skidding into the ditch could be fatal, especially when you were by yourself.

Dawson paid for his food and left the warmth and protection of the restaurant. He needed to think. The moment he set foot outside the door he was forcibly reminded of just how severe the storm was. The air was freezing cold and the wind whipped impenetrable blankets of snow crystals into swirls.

Not good, he thought. *I'll get my wallet from the car and check into the motel. If I end up unemployed, so be it. Better than ending up dead.*

Relieved that he'd made the decision, Dawson walked toward the passenger side of his car to retrieve the wallet he'd left in the glove compartment. As he approached, he was stopped in his tracks by the realization of how bad the visibility really was. Why, it actually looked as though there was someone standing beside the car.

Dawson shook his head but the vision didn't vanish. He jumped when the image called out, "Hello."

"What the…?" he answered, his fists tightening reflexively. "Who are you? What are you doing at my car?"

"Sorry, I didn't mean to startle you. I'm harmless, honest. I'm looking for a ride south toward Edmonton, though. Are you going that way?"

Dawson's heart was still thumping hard enough from the surprise of finding the man standing out in the storm that it took him a minute to consider his answer—which gave the stranger time to add that he had a cell phone with him.

Relief washed over Dawson. How could he be so lucky? He'd get home tonight and to work tomorrow. "I am heading south, and I'd be really glad to have some company for the drive," he said. "By the way, I'm Dawson. What's your name?"

"Richard," the man answered as they finished brushing off the snow that had accumulated on the car in the short time Dawson had been in the restaurant.

"Do folks call you Richard or do you use a nickname like Rick or Rich or something?" Dawson asked, just to make conversation as he steered the car out onto the dark, snow-covered highway.

"No, I go by Richard," the young man answered. "It's sort of a nickname as it is. My full name is Richardson. It was my mother's name before she married my dad."

"Really?" Dawson asked with genuine surprise. "That's a weird coincidence. My name is my mother's maiden name too."

The man in the passenger seat only nodded. He appeared to be drifting off to sleep. Dawson took the opportunity to eyeball the man a bit more closely. They appeared to be about the same age and even much the same height and build. *I wonder what the guy does for a living? And why the heck was he out on the highway tonight?*

He couldn't spend too much time sneaking looks at his companion or even too many seconds wondering about him because he needed to focus on the road ahead. Without a doubt these were the worst driving conditions he could ever remember being out in.

By the time he spotted a roadside sign indicating that the town of Smoky Lake was only a dozen kilometres away, Dawson was uncomfortably aware that the combination of the stressful driving conditions and the sandwich back at the truck stop hadn't agreed with his stomach. *I need a roll of antacids,* he thought with an envious glance at his passenger, who had been in a dead sleep pretty much since they'd started south. *Okay—next exit I'll pull off. I just hope I don't have to drive too far into town to find a store. I'd better hope it's open late, too.*

A faint yellow puddle of light in the distance gave Dawson hope that he'd soon be chewing an antacid tablet or two and that the roads south of Smoky Lake had remained in better shape than the ones he'd just driven over. His passenger was so deeply asleep by now that he was snoring noisily.

Dawson pulled up in front of a convenience store and turned off the ignition in the car, hoping that the change in noise and vibration would waken Richard; he could do with the company. But the man slept on, blissfully unaware of any requests on his being. *Just leave him I guess,* Dawson thought, but as a precaution took the key out of the ignition and tucked it into his jeans' pocket. By the time he came out of the store just a few minutes later, Dawson decided that he'd been paranoid and unkind in not just leaving the car running. The guy had given no indication he was anything but a straight-shooter. Taking the keys really was a bit of an insult. *If he's awake I'll tell him sorry, that it was just habit.*

But Dawson never had that opportunity. By the time he got back to his car, the passenger seat was empty.

"Richard!" he called, thinking that the man must be nearby, stretching his legs and getting some fresh air. The only answer was the whine of the wind through the sentinel of pine trees behind the store.

"Damn, that's inconsiderate of him," Dawson muttered to himself as he made his way back to the store, now figuring that Richard had gone inside and that the two had somehow missed seeing one another.

But when he asked him, the man behind the counter shook his head. "You're the only one who's come in here for more than an hour, son. If I see him, though, I'll let him know you waited a bit for him."

Dawson nodded and made his way back toward his car. Richard was still nowhere to be seen, and Dawson was surprised at how sorry he was that he'd apparently be making this last leg of the trip alone once more, even if the storm had let up considerably and the road looked to be in much better condition. He backed out of his parking spot, moved the transmission lever from reverse to drive—and slammed on the brake. The only footprints in the parking lot were his own. The snow on the passenger's side of the car was thick and deep and completely unmarked—not a footprint in sight. Richard hadn't gotten out of the car so much as he had simply vanished from the car. His parka lay on the car seat, a cell phone on top of that.

This is freakin' impossible, Dawson thought, slamming the car door and stumbling toward the store again.

"What the hell's going on here?" he asked the storekeeper, his voice shaking.

"I can't honestly say I know, son, except to tell you stuff like this has been happening since even before the time I owned this store. I don't rightly know if it's some kind of an altered time/space continuum or a ghost or a guardian angel or quite what's at work here."

"So you've seen this guy Richardson before?"

The man sighed, "I don't know what to tell you. No, I've never seen him in particular. It's an odd thing. I know about him, or them, or it, or whatever the right term should be. It always happens on this stretch of road, and whoever or whatever it is always has something in common with the person who's picked them up. Sometimes it's a man, sometimes a woman. It seems to depend on who the driver is that needs help. It usually happens in the winter, probably just because the roads are the worst then, but once in August a woman came in here all upset. She was diabetic and had neglected to eat before she left Bonnyville. Then some other woman flagged her down just a few kilometres along and asked for a ride. First thing she pulled out of her purse was a full bottle of orange juice that she said she didn't want—something about it not being the brand she liked. It was exactly what the driver needed, just a bit of nourishment to tide her over. They pulled in here so the driver could buy some juice that was more to the other lady's liking, but when she got back to the car the passenger's seat was empty except for the juice bottle."

Dawson shook his head, not wanting to believe either the experience he'd just had or the story he'd just heard. He thanked the man and walked back through the snow to his car. There on the passenger's seat still lay the parka that Richardson had been wearing, with the cell phone on top. He knew he had everything he needed to make the rest of the trip in safety.

What he didn't know was what he'd do if that cell phone ever rang.

Your Salvation

Jeremy had never had much going for him. Even when he was too young to realize it, he never really fit in. His teachers in the small, southern Alberta city where he lived recognized his situation, and many of them did what they could to even out the playing field for him by offering bits of special attention here and there—the kind of attention they knew Jeremy's mother didn't give him.

By junior high the boy had become well aware that he was different from the other kids. For one thing, his clothes were never right. He started school every September with a new pair of jeans—ones that were always way too long for his scrawny legs. By June he'd grown so much that those same jeans were flood pants. There were only ever a couple of weeks, usually sometime in January, when his pants were a reasonable length. But those few days of having perfect-length jeans were usually wasted anyway because he'd have the jeans tucked into snow boots.

While there was little about Jeremy's life that made it good or easy, the boy did have one asset that was uniquely his own. He was a gifted artist. He loved to draw, and he did so very well. His teachers often tried to encourage him by saying, "Your art will be your salvation, Jeremy."

In his final year of high school, the boy's homeroom teacher entered three of Jeremy's paintings in an art contest. First prize was $10,000, which was enough to cover expenses at art college, where he could get the training he'd need to make his way in the world as a professional artist. It seemed that the prediction was true—Jeremy's art would be his salvation.

"This competition is a huge deal," his teacher explained. "It's a juried art show, and it'll be held at the museum. Everyone will be dressed up, so you'll definitely need to wear a suit."

The young man's face fell. He'd never owned a suit in his life. His potential for a successful future seemed to vanish before his eyes. Discouragement washed over him so completely that he barely realized the teacher was still talking.

"I'm going to give you 50 dollars. If you scout the thrift shops around town you'll be able to get what you need."

When Jeremy tried to thank the teacher for his kindness, the man shook his head and said, "I'm happy to be able to help."

The next morning Jeremy tucked the money into his too-short jeans' pocket and took a bus downtown. At the first used clothing store he found a pair of black dress shoes for $10. A block away, where another charity had their thrift store, he found a suit for $30—amazingly it was actually a pretty good fit. Now all he needed to buy was a shirt, and he'd have the proper clothes for the biggest event of his life.

But where could he find a shirt for only $10? A new one was completely out of the question, and he'd been to all the used clothing stores. He needed to think. It was a beautiful day, so in order to clear his head and to save the cost of bus fare, Jeremy decided to walk home.

With each step he took, he felt more and more discouraged. He'd effectively wasted the money that he'd spent because he still didn't have the clothes he needed to attend the show. Perhaps he was foolish to have accepted his teacher's advice. After all, the guy was a chemistry teacher; what did he know about the art world?

Then, around the next corner, Jeremy saw a store he'd never noticed before. It wasn't really a store so much as a place that rented tuxedos. There in the window was a sign that potentially spelled out a solution to his dilemma: "Gently used men's clothing for sale."

Less than 15 minutes later, Jeremy was back on the sidewalk, happily clutching an additional plastic bag. *This shirt is a fabulous bargain,* he thought. *The man even said it's never been worn by another living soul. It's perfect for tonight, and then next year when I'm in art college I can wear it with jeans and completely fit in with what the other guys are wearing.*

As soon as he got home, he carefully laid out the new clothes on his bed. Unfortunately, he had to admit that the suit looked considerably more worn than he'd thought when he bought it. *I guess you can't expect perfection for 30 dollars,* he told himself as he polished his new dress shoes to a gleaming shine.

That evening Jeremy was dressed and ready to leave for the exhibition far too early. He knew his nerves wouldn't let him sit still at home, so he decided to walk to the gallery. He hoped that the fresh air and exercise would help to calm his anxiety.

But the walk didn't have the effect that he'd hoped it would. As a matter of fact, by the time he'd gone a few blocks he felt worse than when he'd left home—a lot worse. Cold sweat beaded on his forehead. His shoes pinched, his suit felt heavy and his shirt collar scratched his neck. He began to feel dizzy, so dizzy that when he reached the art gallery stairs, instead of climbing up them, he gratefully sat on the bottom step and leaned his head against the marble pillar beside it.

And that is exactly where they found the boy's body.

An autopsy revealed that he had been poisoned. Jeremy's mother, perhaps overwhelmed with guilt at having ignored her son for most of his life, was devastated. She couldn't handle any of the particulars that needed to be dealt with, so the task of picking up her son's belongings and the death certificate fell to his teacher.

It seemed that the medical examiner had found a line of scratches and small cuts around Jeremy's neck, as well as toxic residues in his blood stream. Everyone was confused and concerned. Terribly disheartened, the teacher took away the bundle of clothing, deciding that the best thing to do would be to donate the clothes back to the charity stores they had come from.

In the suit jacket pocket he found the receipt for Jeremy's purchase of the white shirt. The man decided to make that his first return. As he entered the store, the town undertaker was leaving—with a bundle of $20 bills clutched in his hand. Inside the store, a large brown paper package lay on the counter beside the cash register.

Suddenly the tragic puzzle pieces fell together in the teacher's mind. The unscrupulous store owner kept his shelves well stocked with the help of an equally unscrupulous undertaker who stripped corpses of their clothes just before burial. It was a wonder that the scheme had not turned deadly before. The man in the tuxedo rental store had not lied to Jeremy. No living soul *had* ever worn that shirt before. It had been taken from an embalmed cadaver, but not until after the cotton had absorbed the poisonous embalming fluid. Then the stiff new collar had scratched Jeremy's neck, allowing the poison into the boy's bloodstream.

And so, Jeremy's kindly and optimistic teachers had been right about his art being his salvation. But they'd been right in the most dreadful way imaginable.

Twin Destinies

"I've never been to a fortune teller before," Mandy admitted nervously as she looked around the small dark room in the back of a building on Canmore's Main Street.

"Then what brings you here today?" the skinny woman seated across from her challenged.

"It's my brother, Gavin, my twin brother. We're orphans. He's my closest friend. He's so terribly sick, and I'm afraid that he'll die. I'll be alone in the world then," Mandy explained.

"I know that, silly girl. I actually am psychic, you know. I'm not one of those charlatans."

Mandy flinched at the anger in the woman's voice. Was it too late to flee? Where was the door? It was too dark to see clearly. She'd only come in a moment ago, but already she was dizzy with disorientation. "I'm sorry, I didn't mean to imply you weren't gifted. But you asked me why I came to see you."

"Your brother has that deadly flu, doesn't he?"

Mandy nodded.

"Well, you don't need to be concerned. I promise that he will outlive you, my worried one," the psychic said with a wave of her hand. "Now go on, get out of here."

Mandy stepped out into the early summer afternoon. The sunshine made her eyes feel dry and scratchy—like her throat had felt all day. Her heart thumped. She swooned and fell to the sidewalk, dead from the flu. The fortune teller had been correct. Mandy's twin brother outlived her, but only by a few hours after being told of his beloved sister's sudden death.

The Grim Reaper's Surprise

Dave has had some memorable days in his life—the day he started his first job, the day he moved out on his own, the day he met his girlfriend—but there was one day that will always stand out over all the rest—and not in a good way.

Dave and his old school friend Andy were working as ranch-hands on a spread near Longview, just southwest of Calgary. On the morning in question, Andy had been up and out of the bunkhouse early, so Dave was surprised to see his friend heading back toward crew's quarters at top speed. Realizing that something must be very wrong for a fellow as laid back as Andy to be running like that, Dave stuck his head out the trailer door. "Whoa, slow down, man. What's up? Why are you running like that?"

Gasping for air, Andy shoved Dave back inside. He tried to talk, but he was panting so hard that he could only manage a word or two at a time.

"Slow down, man," Dave said. "I can't understand a thing you're saying. I thought you just said you saw Death."

Andy gave an exaggerated nod. "I did. I saw Death, but it's worse than just that. He glared at me. I swear he did. If I hadn't run away he would've had me for sure."

"Were you drinking last night? I've never seen you like this. How the heck do you know you saw Death? How do you even know what Death looks like?"

"Are you stupid, Dave? Death! The Grim Reaper! You know what he looks like as well as I do—all dressed in black, carries a sickle. He's ugly, ugly, ugly. He stared at me. It felt as though he could see right through me. Look, give me the keys to your truck. I have to get out of here—now. I'll stay in Calgary tonight. Phone me if he's gone by tomorrow, but even so maybe I'll wait another day before I come back. You won't need your truck anyway because you'll have to be working while I'm gone."

Dave shook his head in concern and pulled his truck keys out of his pocket and handed them to his friend. "You're gone all right—gone crazy if you ask me—but here, take the keys and get out of here if it'll make you feel better. I'll let the boss know that you'll be back in a few days."

That afternoon, Dave was repairing a fence up near the main house when he noticed someone standing down by the creek. He presumed it was a man, only because the person was very tall—and maybe quite thin, he thought at second glance, although it was tough to tell much of anything for sure because of the weird clothes, which were so loose and billowy that it actually looked like the person was wearing a full-length, black robe complete with a hood, of all crazy things on a summer day. This certainly wasn't anyone he recognized.

Knowing that his boss wouldn't take kindly to a trespasser on the property, Dave set down the tools he'd been working with and started toward the creek. It crossed his mind that this might be the person who'd scared Andy, but before he'd had a chance to mull over that possibility, something else grabbed his attention.

Jeez, that can't be the creek that smells that foul, but something sure stinks awful—absolutely rancid, he thought. His stomach lurched at the stench, and he cursed himself for having noticed the stranger in the first place. But there was a chance that this was the guy who'd scared Andy off, and he wanted to defend his friend's honour.

"Hey you, wait right there. I want to talk to you," he called out angrily.

The figure remained motionless. As Dave approached, the warmth seemed to evaporate from the air, replaced by a putrid stench.

Fighting back nausea, he demanded, "Who are you, and why did you scare my friend like that?"

The black hood covering the figure's head moved almost imperceptibly, revealing burning red coals where its eyes should have been. Too late, Dave realized where the dreadful stench came from.

With a voice that sounded like wet wood being ripped through a buzz saw, the figure answered, "I didn't mean to scare him. I was just surprised to see him here. He and I have a date this afternoon in Calgary."

A Little Local Folklore

"I'd love to stay and chat, Linda, but I have that long drive home," Bev Nichols said as the 30-something women made their way from the pottery studio.

"Do you have to leave just yet? It's early. I don't live far from here, and I'm so pumped from the day I've had. It was a great class tonight, plus at work I've been collecting all sorts of old information for a local history book. Some of the photographs are fascinating. I've even found some old pottery kilns. You'll love them. Come to my house for a quick cup of tea before you head for home," the other woman suggested as the two headed toward their cars.

"I can't, I'm sorry. It's getting dark so early these days, and my husband worries about me being on the highway at night," Bev said, climbing into her mini-van and turning on the ignition. She so wanted to accept the woman's invitation, but it wasn't worth risking Terry's ire. It was true that he didn't like her to be out at night, but Bev knew it wasn't because he worried about her driving after dark. It was because he thought she should be home with him.

Forcing a smile, Bev waved to her friend and steered the car out of the parking lot, her smile fading with a sigh. It was time to start the trek home. She'd brought some music to listen to on the drive, but even her favourite tunes didn't seem like a consolation for not being able to join her friend for tea, so she drove in silence. At least the traffic from Lethbridge to Fort Macleod was light, so the drive would be relaxing.

Bev had been surprised at how important her pottery classes had become to her. She could never have anticipated how very much she enjoyed working with the soft, wet clay. Even the thought of the cool, wet mud between her fingers made her smile, and then too there were the other potters at the studio. They were such fun to be with and so supportive. Tuesday evenings had become the highlight of her week—right up until it was time to drive home. Then the tension set in because she never knew what kind of a mood Terry would be in. He was never pleasant, but some weeks were worse than others.

Caught between remembering the fun and satisfaction of the class and anticipating the frustration of having to listen to her husband's selfish indignation, Bev steered around a sharp bend in the highway.

"Oh no!" she screamed.

An elderly man stood right in the path of her car. She yanked the steering wheel to the right and braked so hard that she was nearly standing on the pedal. Something solid bounced against the car's front bumper with a sickening thud. She'd hit the man.

Fighting panic, Bev threw the gearshift lever into park and jumped from the van. *Maybe he's all right. It could have been just a glancing blow,* she told herself. *I'm only a few minutes out of the city and I have a cell phone. Do what needs to be done and stay calm. It'll be all right. It'll be all right.*

"What the…?" Bev stared at the empty road around her van in disbelief. There was no elderly man. There was no body on the road. For that matter, there was no one anywhere within sight. The man she'd seen as clear as could be, the man whose body she'd heard and felt hit her car, simply wasn't there.

She rushed from one side of the road to the other—nothing in either ditch or in the fields beyond. "What have I done? And what should I do now?" Bev whimpered, leaning against the front of her van to keep her weak knees from giving out under her.

Wait a minute, she thought. *My car's not damaged—not even dented.* Bev's heart raced, and her pulse pounded in her ears. The man had been in the middle of the road. He'd been standing directly in front of her van. She'd seen him clearly enough to remember his appearance. He was elderly, tall, thin and balding. Even though she'd braked and swerved as best she could, she knew she'd hit him with a fair amount of force. And yet there was no sign that anything at all had happened.

What should I do? How do I report this? she asked herself as she made her way back to the driver's seat and grabbed for her cell phone. *I don't think this rates a 9-1-1 call—it's hardly an emergency if nothing happened.*

As Bev sat holding the phone with shaking hands, those last words echoed in her mind—nothing happened, nothing happened, nothing happened. Soon, her heart rate slowed.

Well then, if nothing happened then there's nothing for me to do—except of course to finish driving home.

She fumbled to turn on the radio. What she needed was a distraction—something—anything—to hold her concentration from the memory of that man standing in the middle of the highway, the nauseating thump his body made against her van, and the fact that there was no trace of him anywhere. A golden oldies station played a song that reminded Bev of high school, and she made an effort to breathe normally again.

Maybe I just imagined the whole thing. Maybe I didn't hit anyone or even see anyone, she told herself, but that possibility only brought a moment's relief because the implications of having such hallucinations were pretty frightening too. Seeing, and even hitting, a nonexistent pedestrian certainly didn't say anything positive about the state of her mental health. She knew she was stressed about Terry's moods, but surely not so stressed that she was hallucinating.

Just calm down and drive home, she told herself. *You can think things through in the morning.*

The rest of the trip was uneventful, and as she pulled into the driveway, Bev was relieved to see that the house was in darkness. Terry had gone to bed. What a relief. She undressed in the bathroom and climbed into bed so gently that the sleeping man's snores weren't even disturbed. Bev smiled for the first time since she'd left the pottery class. She'd made it. No one would ever have to know what had happened on the way home tonight. *If anything* had *happened,* she thought, relaxing into the welcoming softness of the mattress.

But despite her feelings of relief, Bev couldn't fall asleep. She knew she would be tossing and turning if she had felt free to move. As it was, her fear of wakening Terry was so great that she just lay on her back and stared at the ceiling—where she saw an image of the face of the elderly man she was so sure she had hit staring back at her. By morning, the only way she knew that she'd slept at all was that she'd dreamt of hitting the man on the highway.

At breakfast, Bev tried far too hard to act as though nothing was wrong, which of course made Terry suspicious that something was very wrong.

"You're just acting weird," he told her, stomping into the living room to turn on the television for the weather report.

166 Alberta Fireside Ghost Stories

What if there's news on—some kind of a report about that man I hit? Bev worried, but if there was, her husband didn't mention it.

You didn't hit anyone, she reminded herself firmly, and tried very hard not to wonder why she might have imagined such a thing.

That night Bev drifted off to sleep without any visions. The next morning she was so relieved to be free of the haunting images that she decided to quit the pottery class. *It'll be easier on my nerves if I stay close to home from now on,* she reasoned. *I'll miss it, but I can find another hobby. Being so stressed that I'm actually seeing things that don't exist just isn't worth it for anything.*

Even at the time, part of Bev's mind knew that her reasoning was illogical. She also knew that she needed to reduce her stress level—dramatically. The next evening she would go to the pottery studio to pick up her work and say good-bye to the instructor. Making that decision calmed her, but Bev still felt oddly on edge. She took a deep breath. It was time to leave for work. She locked the door to the house and opened the garage door—where thick tentacles of murky grey mist extended from the rafters and surrounded her van.

Fighting the urge to collapse in a faint of fear, Bev leaned against the garage door frame and gasped for air. Tears coursed down her cheeks. "What's happening to me?" she whimpered.

Slowly Bev inched her way back toward the house. The stairs to the front porch were too much for her, though, and she slumped down onto the first step. She sat with her purse on her lap, huddled in a strange imitation of a fetal position, shaking violently. After a while the shaking lessened. She forced herself to look up and saw a pretty blue sky dotted with white puffy clouds. A perfect spring morning. Nothing looked unusual—no mist or man anywhere to be seen.

I'll just sit here a moment longer. Then I'll go inside and phone the office. There's no way I can handle work today. I'll feel better soon and then I can drive to the pottery studio. I can pick up my pots in the daylight and never have to drive on that highway at night again. On the way home maybe I'll stop at the craft store and treat myself to some supplies for scrapbooking—that's a hobby I can do by myself at home.

Bev steadied herself to stand up and go into the house. A bell ringing somewhere off in the distance startled her, and she grabbed for the stair rail. *Oh great, now I'm hearing things,* she thought, before she realized that it was only the sound of her cell phone ringing in her purse. She made an effort to sound calm as she said hello.

"Bev? Hi, it's Linda. How are you? I'm glad I caught you. I wanted to ask you to come over after work today. Honestly, you have to see these photographs I mentioned, and Tracy, one of the other women working on this local history project I was telling you about, has found a great local legend. It's a ghost story. Can you imagine? Our very own ghost story! They say that years ago an elderly man was killed on the highway just where it curves northbound. His ghost is supposed to haunt that strip of road to this day. They say that if you see him, his spirit never leaves you. How's that for a far-fetched tale, eh? Bev? Bev? Are you there?"

A Murder of Crows

Rudy needed food. It'd been days since he'd put anything but hooch into his stomach. He'd need more of that soon, too, or the shakes would set in fierce. Of course, without the food, the booze wouldn't stay down long enough to kill the shakes. It was always a balancing act. Worse, he wasn't even sure where he was. Still in Grande Prairie for sure, but man, last night must've been a tough one. Hard to remember.

It looked like there was a restaurant just across the street; that would mean good dumpster diving in the alley behind. Getting there would be rough, though. He'd left it too long. He should have eaten yesterday—but no, he couldn't have. Now he remembered, he was sicker than a dog yesterday, which was one of the reasons he felt so bad today. Archie might have meant well sharing that rotgut, but man, it was a bad batch. Just the thought of it made Rudy's stomach heave. He couldn't think of that now—had to get across the street and behind that restaurant.

Walking to the intersection with its assurance of traffic lights was asking too much of his shaky legs. They were quivering so badly it was as though they'd all but given up on the chore of carrying Rudy around from one mess in his life to another. His only alternative was to cross the street from right where he was—in the middle of the block.

He made the step down from the curb to the road hanging onto cars parked on either side of him, but he wouldn't have the luxury of those supports getting across four lanes of traffic. He'd be strictly on his own pegs. He took in as deep a breath as he dared. Nothing to do but step out—right in front of a truck. He made eye contact with the driver just as the man slammed on the brakes. Rudy fell back against the car to his right, scraping his leg on the bumper.

He nodded to the truck driver in what he hoped was a dignified, gentlemanly fashion. He could see the man wipe his brow with one hand and put the other hand out the truck's side window, signalling the driver of the car in the next lane to stop too.

It took all the concentration and energy he could muster, but the next thing Rudy knew he was standing on the yellow line exactly in the middle of the road. He was swaying a bit, but if he could make it the same distance he'd just covered, he'd be on the other sidewalk, right in front of the restaurant. And then, if there was a god, the entrance to the alley would be right beside the restaurant. Rudy didn't think he'd make it much farther than that.

"Hey fella!" the driver in the car next to the truck called. "Are you going to make it across there today?"

Rudy smiled as best he could. He hated what people must think of him. He wanted to tell them that he wasn't always a drunk. He'd had a good life once, a long time ago. Now his life was measured in tottering steps.

He spread his legs to a wider stance for better balance and started off again, staring straight ahead. A few minutes later, crying from the conflicting pains of exertion and relief, he felt the safety of another two parked cars on either side of him. He used them like handrails until he came to the curb. Stepping up to the sidewalk was too much, though. He lowered himself to the curb as best he could but still managed to land hard on his left hip.

Another balancing act—he needed to stay there long enough to catch his breath but not so long that he'd forget why he was there. The restaurant wasn't more than five metres away. Wonderful aromas wafted out the open door and straight from his nose to his stomach. Food. Gotta get to the dumpster. His body's basic need for sustenance—and the nearby lamppost—gave Rudy the strength and the leverage to pull himself up.

And, look at that. There was an entrance to the alley right between the restaurant and the hardware store beside it. The two buildings were close enough together that he could use both walls for balance. He'd make it now.

Ah, this back alley was just the way Rudy liked them: deserted, except for that stupid crow perched on the edge of the garbage bin, an entire crusty bun pinched in its beak. "That's mine," the hungry man muttered angrily as he stooped to grab a piece of concrete that lay nearby, then hurled it with all his adrenalin-fuelled might. His aim was deadly accurate. The bird fell to the pavement, still clasping the leftover. Rudy pulled the bun free of the dead bird's clutches and gnawed on it with greedy delight.

* * *

"I was out for my morning run," the man spoke slowly because the officer seemed to be taking down his words verbatim. "I don't usually come this way, into the alley that is, but like I told the first officer, those crows, they attracted my attention. I've never seen anything like it. There must've been a hundred or more of them in that tree over there. If it'd been spring or summer they wouldn't have been so noticeable, but seeing them all perched there on the bare branches... I have to tell you it was a pretty unusual sight.

Very dramatic—a bit eerie, actually. There were so many of them, they practically covered that old tree. They were absolutely silent and still. The whole world seemed still and silent. Those birds were all staring solemnly in the same direction—just staring. That's why I came back here into the alley. I looked around to see if I could figure out what had their attention, but all I could see that was unusual was a black sheet by the dumpster. Well, not really a sheet, I guess—some sort of a loosely woven fabric. It was pulsing. I'd never seen anything like it. I was trying to figure out what it was when it started to break up, disintegrate I guess. I don't know how to describe it. All the while the birds just continued to perch in the tree, silently staring."

The man stopped for a breath. A film of sweat covered his forehead. He swallowed hard before continuing. "The next thing I saw was the old wino's body there, all chewed and clawed and picked to bits. It was awful. That's why I threw my jacket over him. I don't want it back, by the way. Ever."

The officer looked up from his notepad. "Anything else?"

"Not really. I mean there was a dead crow beside the guy's body, but I don't think that's important, do you?"

Flight to Forever

"This flu is causing as much chaos and anxiety as the Great War that preceded it," Howard said as he walked into the pilot's room at Blatchford Field.

"It seems that way, doesn't it?" Bart, his friend and fellow pilot, agreed. "Are you off up north then?"

Howard nodded. "Fort McMurray this time. The northern settlements are so isolated, but there's an entire plane-load of provisions this time. Should be enough to keep them going for a while."

"There have been reports of heavy fog to the north," Bart cautioned, "so be careful."

"Always am," Howard replied. "I'll be back by midday tomorrow. Meet me at the Selkirk. We'll have lunch and I can tell you about the flight."

Bart offered a distracted wave. It was the best he could do. Jack McCauley, the flight controller, had called to him from the radar bench.

The next morning, Bart headed out early to meet his friend at the Selkirk Hotel. They were both off for the day. That meant no flying, but lots of opportunity to talk about flying—which was almost as good.

Much to his surprise, Bart saw that Howard was already at the restaurant, seated at a table near the window. He hadn't expected him for at least an hour.

"Good to see you," Bart told his friend sincerely. "How was the flight?"

"It was a tricky one, I'll tell you. Lots of fog," Howard replied.

"Well, as long as you managed, that's all that matters because it's my turn to buy lunch."

"Order for me, will you?" Howard asked as he stood up and headed to the back of the room where the washrooms were located.

Bart ordered two bowls of beef stew and waited for his friend to return. When the server brought the steaming plates, he set them down carefully. Then, before turning to leave the table, the waiter paused. "Maybe it's not my place, but I know that you and Howard were good friends. I just wanted to say how sorry I am for your loss."

"My loss? What do you mean, 'my loss'?" Bart asked.

"Jack was in this morning for breakfast—Jack McCauley. He told me about the crash. The fog was so thick that poor Howard apparently never had a chance."

The Shadow of
the Hanging Tree

Folks—strangers to Redcliff County mostly—would shake their heads and marvel at how old the tree was. "It must have been cared for," they'd say, but even so you could see that none of them ever wanted to look at the tree for too long, and when they turned away it was obvious that they felt uncomfortable. Somehow they must have known on some level that it wasn't care keeping the gnarled old thing coming back after every harsh prairie winter.

No sir. Care is loving. Something much, much darker nurtured the hanging tree, and no one knew that as well as Gilbert McGibbon. After all, his property butts up hard against the county line—the no-man's land where that oak put down roots more years ago than anyone can remember. Even as a youngster growing up on the farm, Gilbert knew it was best to ignore the twisted old tree—and he did. But when he saw the sold sign on the neighbouring spread, the first thing he thought of was the hanging tree. He wondered who had been foolish enough to buy that farm and if it was worth warning the person to stay clear of the evil old tree. On the one hand letting the newcomer find out for himself seemed flat-out cruel, but on the other hand Gilbert didn't want to risk being called a nut for talking to a complete stranger about a haunted oak tree.

Gilbert looked toward the west where the sun was setting just beyond the tree's misshapen trunk. Deep down he knew there could be no compromises where this decision was concerned. He'd either have to tell all or nothing and let fate fall out where it may. His new neighbour would hear the story eventually anyway. Someone in town would bend his ear. That's just the kind of regard people have for the oak's power. And not just sensitive people, either. Even the county's toughest hooligans always chose any place but that one for their rowdy bush parties because once twilight has blanketed the landscape, none of the locals want to be anywhere near that tree.

The passage of time had meant that truth and tale had mingled into a story stew. He wondered if he should tell his new neighbour about the ugly old mutt that once lived on that property. About how that dog would happily tag along anywhere his master went, unless the man ventured too close to the tree. Then it was more than evident that the animal had a distinct comfort zone—one that didn't include proximity to that tree. The farmer never understood how or even what it was his dog sensed near the old oak. For the most part the man just kept his distance too.

But what about the new owner? What if he had a family? It was almost a rite of passage for the town's teenagers to torment the younger kids by invoking threats of being captured and taken to the tree. Gilbert didn't think he could add to the children's cruelty by not at least giving a warning.

A few years ago, the story of the tree spread so far that a gaggle of arborists, a forester and even a few tree huggers came out to take a look but, as far as anyone in the area knew, nothing much came of their visits, and none of the city slickers ever returned. After that, Gilbert recalled, some paranormal investigators took their turn visiting. That group had a little more luck—if you could call it that. Exact details of their experience have been lost over the years, but everyone recalls that they left the area pretty quick and pretty scared. They never returned either.

As he thought about the decision facing him, Gilbert scuffed the dry soil with his work boot. He wasn't a man who was comfortable either with making decisions or with talk. Maybe he should just cut to the chase and tell his new neighbour that when the evening light is just right and you stand at a certain angle from the tree, you can see the manifestation of a limp corpse hanging, suspended from a rope that's no longer visible. The air around the hideous image is permeated with fury so intense that it seems to freeze the air. Fleeing is next to impossible. Even breathing is tough.

But then the vision is gone, and there's only an aura around the tree—an aura of evil.

Gilbert also knew the origin of the evil. Way back, decades ago, that quarter section was homesteaded. The story went that the original settler said he'd discovered one of his hired hands—a particularly lazy one—badly beaten. The injured man died before help arrived. Locals were loath to think that anyone in the community might be guilty of such a vicious act.

By coincidence, that very morning, a stranger had the tragically bad fortune to drift into the area. He was an odd fellow, everyone agreed. Gilbert had known a few like that himself—those who just have an odd way about them. Even at the time, everyone around said this stranger had shifty eyes.

The men in the neighbourhood got together a posse, but from what Gilbert had heard, they were more like a group of vigilantes. As quick as that, they captured the unsuspecting transient. Later the same day they tried him and found him guilty. The man protested his innocence, but by nightfall his corpse was swinging from a jerry-rigged noose tied to a young, strong oak tree growing at the boundary of the settler's property.

The stranger's dying words were not a confession but threats and curses upon his captors. The townspeople were glad he was gone, but everyone was also frightened of that homesteader. They knew he was capable of terrible violence. Oddly, he didn't live long after that. His wife found him near the oak tree at the edge of their property—stone cold dead. No cause of death was ever determined.

Gilbert sighed. He knew what he had to do. He'd tell the newcomer everything. But not tonight. He'd tell him during the day, with his back to that vile old tree.

4
Last
Quarter

A Grave Sighting

Until just a few years ago, an old farmhouse stood on a few acres of land near the border city of Lloydminster. The house and the land surrounding it were owned by a man named Jacob Walton. Now Walton was a strange sort of a fellow. To the best of anyone's knowledge he never held a job, and he certainly didn't work his farm. He rarely went into town, and when he did he was decidedly unsociable.

"Of course, that's fine in itself," Big Al, who owned the hardware store, always maintained. "Lots of people aren't talkative. But it does strike me as odd that he always has enough money to buy whatever he needs, and he always pays for those things with 20-dollar bills."

Despite the oddities, everyone pretty much just took Walton's ways for granted and got on with their own lives. That is, they did until a young policeman named Cameron Weir was transferred to the local detachment. After chatting with a few of the community's shopkeepers, including Al at the hardware store, Cam decided that he wasn't happy with this long-standing policy of benign neglect where Walton was concerned.

"How can anyone obviously not work and yet have such a stash of money? There must be something illegal going on. He's gotta be dealing drugs, sarge," the constable said. "I think we should investigate him."

"Suit yourself," the older man said in a tone of voice that indicated an attitude somewhere between exasperation and resignation.

That very afternoon the constable drove out to Walton's farm, but once he got there he found the gate across the man's driveway closed and locked. He called out a few times and saw a tattered curtain move in one of the windows, but other than that the strange old man didn't reply.

Cam thought of climbing over the fence, but the yard was so dirty and overrun with junk that he knew his uniform would be a mess by the time he knocked on the door, and he didn't figure that would present a very dignified image of the police force. *Next time I'll phone first,* he decided, but when he ran that idea past his superior officer, reality interfered.

"Old Walton doesn't have a phone," the sergeant said, barely looking up from his paper work.

"What about a search warrant then?" the constable asked.

"What possible grounds do I have for issuing a search warrant? The guy hasn't done anything except make you curious. I don't think that's a legitimate reason to intrude on a man's privacy."

Cam saw that the sergeant was right and let the subject drop. As he settled into his new posting, he began to adopt the locals' attitude and rarely thought about the odd man who lived alone at the edge of town; even when he did, it was almost fondly and certainly not as a possible drug dealer.

When December rolled around, it was time for the young man's annual leave. He was looking forward to spending the Christmas holidays with his family in the Maritimes and telling them all about his life on the prairies.

While Cam was away, a farmer driving by Walton's place saw the old man slumped on the front porch. The farmer stopped his truck, hopped over the fence and found that

Jacob Walton had died as he had lived—completely alone. The town librarian tried to trace any kin Walton might have but couldn't find a soul. By the time the constable came back from vacation, the hermit had been buried in a corner of the cemetery and people had gone back to tending to their own lives. The death of the reclusive man with his mysterious supply of money was of so little consequence to everyone that not a soul thought to mention it to Cam when he came back from his vacation.

His first evening back at work as he patrolled the outlying area of his jurisdiction, Cam drove by the Walton property as he had been doing on every night shift for nearly a year. This time, though, something caught his eye. There was a light flitting about the farmhouse windows. First one window would be lit, and then another and then another.

Looks like there's more than one person in that house. I'd better check this out. Cam steered his cruiser off the dirt road. The gate across the driveway was not only unlocked but also standing wide open. Carefully he made his way along the cluttered path and up to the house. He knocked on the door and called out, identifying himself and asking if anything was wrong. When there was no response he tried the door. It opened with a squeak.

"Hello!" he called out. "Mr. Walton? It's Constable Weir. Are you in here, Mr. Walton? Do you need any help?"

A movement and a flicker of light from deep inside the house caught his eye. Thinking that burglars were lurking, he lowered his hand to his holster. A second later, though, he was relieved to see that it was only Old Man Walton himself wandering about his house with a candle in his hand.

"Hello there," the constable said. "I'm sorry to seem to break in on you, it's just that your door was unlocked and I was afraid you needed some help. Are you all right, Mr. Walton?"

But the old man paid no attention and continued to scurry about, muttering incoherently to himself as he did. The officer stood quietly, trying to think of what his next move should be.

"Can I help you?" Cam asked. "If you've lost something, my flashlight might help. It casts a lot more light than your candle."

But still the man didn't reply. He didn't even appear to have heard the young man.

"It's freezing in here," Cam continued. Walton just turned down the hall and disappeared into a darkened doorway, muttering all the while. Wanting to be helpful, the policeman started to build a fire in the kitchen hearth. Just as he struck a match to light the kindling, Cam heard a dreadful cackle echoing down the hall.

"Did you say something, Mr. Walton?" the young constable called out, not wanting to intrude any further on the privacy that the man so obviously wanted. "Have you found what you were looking for?"

When there was no answer, the policeman shined his light down the hallway. He could see three doorways leading from the corridor, but all was dark and quiet. Slowly, he made his way toward the first door and pushed it open. The room was full of old newspapers and dusty boxes. "Mr. Walton?" Cam called.

There was no response. He turned to look into the room across the hall but found that it was little more than a closet and was stacked full of boxes. He drew in a deep breath. The man had to be in the end room. *I didn't mean to corner him; I hope he's not too ornery,* Cam thought as he flashed his light into what was clearly the man's bedroom.

But no one was there. Cam shone his light into all the corners. He was ready to turn and leave the room when he noticed that the window was open. "I'll close that for you," he said out loud to the empty room, but the moment he took a step across the floor he noticed something: there were boot tracks across the dusty floor leading to the open window. Cam's heart sank. He'd come in to try to help the man but instead had scared him and made him flee from his own house through deep snow in the dead of winter. The officer left the house feeling dejected that his attempt at a good deed had gone so badly.

Before heading back to his cruiser, Cam walked around the outside of the house. The old man certainly wasn't anywhere to be seen, but there were tracks in the snow from the window in that end room that led straight to the old wooden fence dividing Walton's property from the churchyard. More convinced than ever that the old eccentric needed help, the constable jumped the fence and followed the trail of footprints into the graveyard and around the snow-shrouded headstones. The tracks ended at a plain wooden cross near a corner of the cemetery.

The guy must be so scared that he's hiding from me, Cam thought. *I'll bet he's dealing drugs and that's why he ran, but I sure don't want to be responsible for an old man freezing to death.*

"Mr. Walton," Cam called again. "I'm concerned about you. Could you please just let me know that you're all right?

There's a fire all ready to light in your kitchen hearth, so the house should be warm in no time. I'm sorry if I chased you out on this cold night. I didn't mean to."

The constable stood still and listened as intently as he could, but the only sound he heard was a nearby owl hooting. Realizing that his presence was only making the situation worse, he drove back to the police station to wait for his sergeant to come to work in the morning.

"I never thought I'd say this, sarge, but I feel so badly about disturbing Walton," Cam told his boss.

"Well then, I guess I have good news and bad news for you," the older man said as he poured himself a large mug of coffee. "You couldn't have disturbed Jacob Walton. You couldn't even have seen him.

"With all due respect sir, I know I saw him, and he sure reacted like I'd disturbed him," the constable said.

"Son, I'm sorry to inform you that you absolutely could not have seen Jacob Walton last night. The man died while you were away visiting your family. He's buried under a wooden marker at the corner of the cemetery alongside the church."

Constable Cameron Weir grabbed onto his desk for support. There was no way his sergeant was the type of man to tease. Obviously last night he had seen a ghost—a ghost who vanished at exactly his own gravesite.

Years later, when the people of the community finally decided that it was time to tear down the dilapidated farmhouse, they found hundreds of $20 bills hidden in every one of the dozens of boxes that Walton had stored in the place. Everyone had their own opinion on how the hermit came to be so wealthy. Some said he'd been a Chicago gangster in the 1920s. Others said he was born to money and simply hated people. Likely no one will ever know the truth.

Cam Weir, however, is absolutely certain of one thing—that on a cold January night, he saw the ghost of Jacob Walton searching for the cash he left behind.

Getting Home

Somewhere off in the distance, a coyote howled. Nick rubbed his hands across his face to bring himself awake. Oddly, he didn't know where he was. What he did know was that he felt terrible. His lips were dry, his head ached, his eyelids felt like sandpaper and he was cold—very cold.

He sat up and was immediately sorry that he had. Searing pain shot through his back. He slouched and the pain eased a bit. He looked around but couldn't make any sense of his surroundings. Ice-cold water rippled across his legs. Why was he lying at the edge of a river? Then he remembered. Every grim detail flooded his mind, slamming ugly reality into his consciousness.

How long had he been here? And wait—where was Jeff? The brothers had been hiking around the old mine site, and Jeff had been just ahead on the trail when the rain started. Nick had slipped and lost his footing. Looking up, he realized he'd fallen a good 25 metres. That and the boulder he'd landed against would explain why his back hurt so much.

Great, now how do I get home? Jeff must have gone for help. Maybe the best thing is just to wait here, thought Nick. But where was "here?" Nothing looked at all familiar—maybe because it was so dark.

Moonlight cast rippling shadows on the rocks and the leafless trees. The coyote howled again. Nick swore. *Hurry up, will you, Jeff? I can't hang in here too much longer. Gotta move before I freakin' freeze to death.*

Slowly, painfully, the young man pulled himself clear of the river and stood up. *So cold. Can hardly make my legs work.*

The back's not as bad as I thought, though. I'll make it, he told himself.

Like a drunk stumbling along an unfamiliar path, Nick concentrated on putting one foot in front of the other, not really sure where he was headed. His only goal was to put as much distance as possible between himself and the river, but judging distance was tricky and his legs weren't working right. Each step took more energy than he had left in him. *Legs must be numb from the cold water,* he thought. *This ain't workin'. I'll never make it.*

"Jeff!" Nick called as loud as he was able. "Jeff, where are you? I need you. Jeff! I'm not kidding this time. You gotta come get me."

Tears coursed down his unshaven cheeks. His voice reduced to a whimper, he implored someone, anyone, to help him. *Not ready to die. Don't wanna die.* The exertion had exhausted him completely, and he collapsed onto the ground. *Gotta rest.*

"Of course you do, Nick. Just rest for a while and you'll feel better."

Nick looked up. A young woman stood beside him. *She looks familiar, even the clothes she's wearing. I feel like I know her. But who is she? I can't remember.* "Sorry," he stammered. "I should know who you are. I would for sure, but I've just had a helluva fall and I can't find my brother."

The woman nodded and smiled. Her gaze spread warmth through Nick's body.

She held out her hand. He took it and stood more easily this time. *I still can't quite bring her name to mind.* Everything about her looked so familiar, but something about her didn't seem right. "I have to get home," he said. The woman nodded.

The next thing he knew, Nick was standing outside the house in Cochrane where he and Jeff had lived all their lives. How did he get there? Had he dozed off? He'd read about that once—soldiers so tired from marching that they had actually fallen asleep between steps.

Nick let himself in and stood in the hallway. Where was that woman who had helped him at the river? Why couldn't he remember who she was or where he knew her from? *You must have banged your head pretty bad, loser. Maybe you aren't the sharpest knife in the drawer, but thinking has never been this hard for you before.*

Then it occurred to him. "Grandma!" he said out loud. "That was Grandma who came to help me. Dad had a picture of her from when she was young. She was even wearing the same clothes just now as she was years ago when that picture was taken."

Nick shook his head. His grandmother had been dead for five years. He looked into the living room and saw Jeff sitting alone with his face buried in his hands. Their graduation photos were on the mantel where they'd always been, but now Nick's stood on a black scarf.

"Jeff!" he called. "Sheesh, man. What's happening here?"

But even as Nick spoke, the image of his brother faded from his sight.

"Don't go!" Nick yelled. "Oh no, you're dead, aren't you? It was your ghost that I saw sitting there, wasn't it? Oh man, I'm sorry. You have no idea how sorry I am. I would have looked for you, but I thought you'd already made it out okay. I'll never forgive myself until the day I die."

"Come with me, now," the young woman who would be—or had been, which was it?—his grandmother held out her hand to him again.

All the sorrow and pain drained from Nick's body as he put his hand in hers. He'd been wrong. His brother wasn't dead. He hadn't seen Jeff's ghost. In utter bliss Nick watched as the house, the yard, the neighbourhood, the city and then the earth itself receded. His soul sighed contentedly.

Groan

Jennifer knew she shouldn't have stayed so late at the party. Okay, for that matter she shouldn't even have gone to the party at all, but heck, there weren't that many parties in Rocky Mountain House, and with her parents away for the weekend, well, it just seemed too good an opportunity to pass up.

She knew it would be tough to get up in the morning and go to her Saturday babysitting job. She also knew her guilty conscience would torment her. Her parents had trusted her to manage on her own in a mature way, and she'd *so* betrayed that trust by going to the party in the first place and then by staying out so late. Why had she thought it would be fun, especially when the other girls brought out that ouija board? That wasn't fun at all. It was downright creepy. Someone must have been making the weird groaning sound that was supposedly from the spirit they had contacted. Plus, Lynne's parents mustn't ever turn the heat on in that basement. It was freezing down there.

Jennifer began to walk faster just to warm up. It would get her home quicker too, and that was where she wanted to be, very badly, right now. Soon she was jogging.

"Just gotta get home," she told herself out loud. "If I cut through the park, that'll save a bit of time," and she veered off the sidewalk and onto the dew-damp grass.

She was past the empty and forlorn-looking swings, slides and teeter-totters when she remembered that the pioneers' graveyard was just over the fence. She shivered as though it were ice water, not blood, running through her veins. *Suck it up, dumb-dumb. It's not even a real graveyard. There's just one monument, and no one really even knows how many graves were ever there or even where each one is.*

Promising herself never to do anything like this again, Jennifer hurried through the darkened park—until something grabbed her ankle. She screamed and reached down to free herself.

No one had grabbed her. She'd just caught her foot on a protruding root. She gave a little nervous laugh and started on her way through the darkness again. Fog swirled around her. Sounds echoed strangely. An owl seemed to hoot first from one tree but then from another. For a while it even sounded as though someone was following her. That couldn't be, she told herself. There couldn't be anyone else here, not at this hour. But there was that groaning again, just like at the séance. "I just want to be home," she whimpered.

Jennifer's hands were shaking so badly by the time she reached her front door that she could barely get the key into the lock. Finally she pushed her way inside the house and slammed the door. Her relief was so intense that it rendered her unable even to think. She ran up the stairs to the security of her bedroom—it was ice-cold. She covered her ears. Anything not to hear the groans coming from under her bed.

An Erratic Destiny

"The others in the dorm had a strange conversation last night. Some of them were discussing the possibility that there's life after birth. Have you ever heard any talk about such a thing?" Yar asked his soulmate as they sat together on the huge rock.

At first Mik didn't answer but simply stared out at the fields of wheat swaying in the prairie breeze. When she did begin to speak, Mik's tone was serious and her voice was low. "I've heard souls speculate about such mysteries, but frankly, their talk always makes me uncomfortable. And besides, it doesn't concern us now. My Greeter assured me that you get warnings when you're about to be born. She said you feel different, strangely solid somehow. Almost as though you exist in a physical body. It's just too alien a concept for me to understand, I'm afraid."

Yar's ethereal form indicated that he'd heard his beloved Mik's thought, but other than that he didn't respond. Mik's words and the words of the souls in the dorm where he rested were frightening to him. Could his impending birth account for the heaviness he'd been feeling? Yar loved Mik with all his vaporous being. Leaving her behind was too difficult a concept to bear. "You're right, Mik. It's not nice to think about. Let's go back to just being."

In time, Yar, Mik and all the other souls returned to their quarters. It never crossed their minds to say goodbye or even good night to one another, for they were always apart for rest and always together while awake. It had been that way forever and *would* be that way forever.

As Yar went to his cubicle, the oldest soul in the quarters approached him. "You won't be resting here anymore. You're leaving us. Your birth is only a few moons away."

Yar heard the respected elder's message with terror and disbelief. It couldn't be. He wasn't ready to be born. He still had so much being that he wanted to do. As he watched the old soul retreat, Yar thought, *So this is definitely why I've been feeling odd for the last little while. And this must be why the others were speaking of such strange events as the possibility of life after birth and what might happen to a soul after birth.*

He tossed and fidgeted. His shapeless form was definitely changing, and those changes weren't comfortable. Seconds later, something far more uncomfortable struck Yar. *Mik! I need to tell her what's going to happen. How can I leave her? Our rock. Our waves. We're two halves. We always have been. We aren't complete without one another. She will be so sad and worry herself sick. Some people say that sadness and worry alone can bring on a premature birth.*

When it was time for the elder soul to check the dorm of resting beings once more, he passed Yar's cubicle and said quietly, "We all have to be born sometime, Yar. There's love in life too, I understand."

Yar didn't hear the old soul's last sentence. He had already left to join his happily expectant parents.

* * *

Nine months later, Margaret and Raymond Robertson were delighted at the birth of their bouncing baby boy. They named him Raymond after his father, but henceforth, and with great pride, always called the boy Ray.

Little Ray was a bright child. Everyone who knew him remarked on his intense curiosity. He always seemed to be looking for something. "Maybe tomorrow," he would often tell his parents when they tucked him into bed at night.

"What does he mean?" Raymond and Margaret wondered, but for years they felt he was too young to be able to explain.

The night before the lad's 10th birthday, when he once again uttered that same, odd phrase, Ray's mother asked him for an explanation. "What might be tomorrow, son?"

"I might find it tomorrow," the child replied with finality.

Still every bit as puzzled, Margaret kissed Ray, tucked him in, wished him a good night and reminded him that when he woke up the next day he'd be 10 years old.

Although Ray's 10th birthday was a wonderful time for him, he apparently did not find what he was searching for because at bedtime the boy again muttered the words "maybe tomorrow."

When Ray repeated the phrase on the eve of his 11th birthday, his curious mother once again asked him what it was he meant by those words. This time, however, with a year's additional maturity, he was able to answer a bit more fully.

"Maybe tomorrow I'll find my best friend."

Margaret was surprised to hear this explanation. "But, Ray, you have a best friend. Larry's your best friend. You two are always together."

Ray looked up at his bewildered mother and replied, "No. My best friend is a girl. I'll find her."

Mother and son stared at one another in silence. Seconds later Ray's eyes closed and Margaret made her way toward the bedroom door. As she reached the hallway outside the boy's room she was sure she heard him say, "Maybe tomorrow."

* * *

Kim, always reserved, seemed fully resigned to being left alone frequently. Her father often said that the child had a maturity far, far beyond her years, but then really that wasn't very surprising. Her parents were in their late forties by the time Kim's mother found she was pregnant. They were delighted by the surprise and adored their little girl, but by then they'd established a pleasant, but quiet, life for themselves—one that they actively guarded. As a result, the little girl had an upbringing that was both privileged and yet at the same time, deprived. Casual acquaintances were sure that this was why she was such an unusual child. Those who knew the situation better, however, realized that there was something even more fundamental at work here. It wasn't just her family background that made Kim different. Her essence was also different.

Since she'd been a toddler, Kim had been fascinated with rocks. As she grew older she began collecting and categorizing rocks, almost to the point of obsession. Over the years many people asked about this passion of hers, but try as she might, Kim couldn't adequately explain her interest and usually ended up just telling folks that rocks somehow represented something essential to her.

In high school, during spring break, Kim's science class took a weeklong field trip to the Rocky Mountains. No one had ever seen Kim happier. She enjoyed the days of scouting out different rock formations and the evenings of campfires and ghost stories, but mostly she enjoyed sleeping outside, with the star-studded sky as her roof. The thought of going back home to the city nearly broke her heart. Fortunately, the teacher had even planned interesting stops for the drive home—including time to explore the Okotoks erratic, just southwest of Calgary.

196 Alberta Fireside Ghost Stories

As the bus pulled off the road near the enormous rock, Kim gasped. "There it is," she whispered. "That's our rock."

"What's wrong?" the girl sitting next to her asked. "You've gone all white."

"Let me out of here. I have to get off the bus. Now!"

Pushing her way through the crowd of her classmates in the aisle of the bus, Kim barely breathed until her feet were on the gravel path leading to the huge boulder that a glacier had dropped in its wake during its ice-age retreat.

"What's wrong with Kim?" her former seatmate persisted. "Mr. Harris, I think there's something wrong with Kim."

But they were wrong. There was nothing wrong with Kim. Finally she'd found what she'd been searching for her entire life.

* * *

"Larry's parents asked me to go on a picnic with them. Can I?" Ray asked.

"May I," his mother corrected.

"Whatever. I want to go, 'kay?"

Smiling, Margaret nodded. It was the last day of spring break, and the young man had spent his days away from school cleaning and painting the basement of their house. He deserved to get away into the country before school re-opened.

That afternoon, the teenaged boys sat quietly in the backseat of Larry's parents' van. Usually Ray was the more talkative of the two friends, but today he was uncharacteristically quiet. He didn't even react to the chaos on the road when the traffic had to slow down and pull over as an ambulance sped by with its siren blaring. In the confusion, a truck sideswiped the car ahead of them, spun around and smashed into the van, hitting it just behind the driver's door.

Later Larry tried to console Ray's mother by assuring her that he was positive her son hadn't had as much as a moment of fear because even at the moment of the fatal impact, he hadn't reacted at all. His words were effective—Larry could see that his friend's mother was at least somewhat consoled, and that was the reason he never told anyone that he distinctly remembered seeing a smile spread across his friend's face just seconds before the impact crushed the life from Ray's young body.

* * *

Kim had scrambled to the top of the enormous rock too fast for anyone to catch up to her. Her classmates were barely halfway between the bus and the base of the erratic by the time she'd climbed to the very top of it. Only one boy was near enough to the rock to see her fall to her death. Years later he still wasn't able to wipe the memory of her smiling, dead face from his mind.

To Find His Fortune

"I promised my family I'd be back for them as soon as I'd found my fortune, but that was back in 1933, and I'm no closer to finding it now than I was then," Clem told his two companions as they settled around an early evening campfire. He hoped that the tone of his voice hadn't revealed his anger and frustration. Even more, though, he hoped he'd be safe for the night. The newly formed trio had chosen a spot at the edge of the hobo jungle. They knew they needed to be near the railway tracks, but they also knew that arguments among the homeless, unemployed men could break out at the slightest provocation and that even the most minor disagreements could quickly turn deadly.

"Our Uncle Clarence, God rest his soul, once spoke exactly those words," Walter said.

"Hah! I doubt that God is anywhere near old Clarence's soul. That man was one hateful cuss," Walter's brother Norm retorted. "Besides, I always thought that miserable uncle of ours said it was his fate, not his fortune he was after."

Clem didn't give two hoots about their uncle's fate *or* his fortune, but he did have a keen interest in keeping the two brothers from scrapping, so he chose his next words carefully and with an eye to smoothing things over.

"Well, you can't blame your uncle for wanting to improve his lot, whether it was his fate or his fortune he was seeking. Almost anything's better than not being able to support your family—unless, of course, it's this life, moving from one camp to another and sleeping with one eye open to make sure the other tramps don't steal what little you have left," Clem said. "Where did your uncle's search take him, any idea?"

Norm shook his head. "Don't rightly know. I reckon it couldn't have been far from here, though, because he spent his whole life around here in the Sylvan Lake area," he explained. "I doubt he'd ever venture much farther afield."

Walter said, "I do remember. He found something near here, just the next town over, actually—with a man called Pardelli."

The next town over? An unfamiliar sensation rose in Clem's chest. It took him a moment to recognize the feeling. It was hope. His definition of what his fortune might consist of had changed drastically over the past couple of years. At this point the possibility of three meals a day and a roof over his head at night sounded so appealing that he jumped up. "What are we waiting for? Let's set out to find this man Pardelli."

Norm shot his brother a look. Walter shrugged. "It's as good an idea as any, I guess," he said.

"If we can get work there, we might never have to see a hobo jungle again for the rest of our lives," Clem declared to the other two men once they'd walked a safe distance away from the camp. His companions nodded. Ironically, the three men were unaware that the ravages of the Great Depression had pummelled their self-respect and dignity at least as badly as it had those of the men whose company they'd just fled.

It wasn't long before Clem, Walter and Norm found Pardelli's farm on the outskirts of the neighbouring town.

"You heard right," the man told them tersely. "I can give you work and pay you in cash, but you'll have to take care of feeding yourselves. Got no woman here to cook for y'all.

And one more thing: if any others come looking for work, you'll have to share the chores and the wages with them."

All three men were pathetically eager to accept the arrangement. They huddled together to make plans quickly in case the farmer changed his mind.

"Clem, you go into town and get us some grub. Me and Norm will stay here and make sure no one else gets to Pardelli before we prove what good workers we are."

The brothers smiled as Clem set out for town. They all knew that getting food was not an easy task—not without money, anyway, and that was something none of them had had for months. They were pleased that they had been able to push that task onto Clem.

The town was several kilometres away, and as he walked, Clem had plenty of time to consider his next move. It would have been easier if they had all come into town together because then two could divert the shopkeeper's attention by pretending to start a fight in the back of the store while the third pocketed enough food for a few days; the ploy had worked many times for others. The more he walked and the more he thought about being sent on his own, the angrier Clem got. By the time he set foot in the store, his anger had given birth to a plan. He'd not only steal food but he'd steal some poison too. Then on the walk back to Pardelli's he would eat his share and work the poison into the food he set aside for the brothers. If he proved himself to the landowner, he might be able to send for his wife to join him.

But he wasn't the only one of the three plotting. Norm and Walter had decided that as soon as Clem came back with the food, they would kill him and hide his body. That way the work at Pardelli's would be all theirs.

An hour later the trio was reunited.

"Were these buns the best you could do?" Walter complained when he saw what Clem had brought.

"'Fraid so," Clem replied.

"There's a funny taste to them," Norm added.

"Tasted fine to me," Clem answered.

"I'm throwing mine away," Walter said as he hurled his food several metres away from where he sat.

Clem jumped up to get the poisoned bun. He couldn't run the risk of any of Pardelli's animals eating it and dying. He'd be sure to be blamed. But Clem had gone no more than a few steps when his world went black. Norm had picked up a rock and levelled a fatal blow to the back of his head.

"Hah, now we have the food and all the work to ourselves," Norm said, taking another bite of his bun.

"I'm not feeling so well," Walter said, clutching his stomach.

Norm looked over at his brother for a moment but quickly diverted his gaze to the side. "Uncle Clarence, what are you doing here?" he asked in a small, confused-sounding voice.

A shimmering, slightly transparent form shook with a hollow laugh. "You just never know who will be next to find their fate at Pardelli's," the ghost said before floating away from sight.

'Twas the Week After Christmas

I hate that week between Christmas and New Year's. It's just a weird time. The whole world feels as though it's in the doldrums, waiting for one last blow-out party before life goes back to normal, which, in Alberta, consists of slogging through the remaining months of winter. That's why one particular year I decided to take off to Marmot on Boxing Day even though none of my buddies could join me until the end of the week. Little did I know that by the time that day came, I'd have been more than grateful for the doldrums.

The day I left the city it felt wonderful to be in the car and heading out of town. The Yellowhead Highway was all but deserted, and the sky was as clear a blue as it can only be on an Alberta winter day. Better still, it wasn't even all that cold out.

Less than four hours later I checked into the resort long enough to drop my suitcase, grab my skis and get to the hill in time for the last run of the day. It was wonderful, exhilarating. What a great way to avoid moping around and feeling awful for days. The other people riding in the shuttle bus with me from the slopes back to the parking lot must've wondered about the idiot with the silly grin on his face. But I couldn't help it. I was as pleased as the dickens with myself for having come up with this plan to escape from the city at its worst time.

Rather than risk not getting a big enough place for all of us once the weekend came, I'd rented an entire chalet. That meant I'd have everything to myself for at least four days—the fireplace, the hot tub, the whole thing. This was going to be great.

But I hadn't been in the place more than half an hour after coming back from the slopes when I noticed that my mood had started to slip. Maybe I was a bit bored or I was just tired from the drive. Whatever, I decided to make my way up to the loft and hit the sack for the night even though it was really early.

I fell asleep right away, but I couldn't stay asleep for more than a few minutes at a time. I finally figured out that the place was freezing, so I went back downstairs and cranked the thermostat way up. Once all my friends arrived I figured I wouldn't have to do that because the heat from another nine bodies would help keep the place warm. Plus, having them around would mean there'd be lots going on to distract me from thinking old-lady thoughts like being chilly.

It seemed like the place was warming up but I still couldn't sleep, this time because I was hearing noises as if tree branches were scraping against the windows. That struck me as odd because I didn't remember seeing any trees near the place. By morning I'd barely had any sleep at all, but still I decided to hit the slopes and get in as many runs as I could. Not only did I want to ski but I also wanted to make sure that I really tired myself out so I wouldn't have the same problem sleeping again.

I kept skiing as long as I could, but even though I stopped for an early lunch, I barely lasted until 2:00 before heading back to the chalet. Once I was there, it hit me that I should have stayed and hung out at the hill because there sure wasn't anything to do at the resort. I even tried reading one of the old Mickey Spillane pocket books that were stacked on top of the mantle, but it was as boring as any other of his books I'd tried to read, so I decided to go for a walk. An hour out, an hour back should give me a pretty good stroll, I figured, and off I went. Anything to get myself tired enough to fall asleep and stay asleep instead of tossing and turning and lying awake like I'd done the night before.

But that plan didn't work either. Oh, I was tired all right, but it was so cold in the little cabin that I had to take blankets off the other beds and pile them on mine. That kept me warm enough to sleep, but the stupid scraping noise was so loud that it kept me awake. By 4:30 in the morning I'd pretty much given up hope of getting any sleep. I went downstairs, put on the coffee and decided to wander out to main part of the resort to pick up a newspaper.

There was a light on in the chalet next to mine. A woman was standing at the front window looking out. I waved to her. I was so desperate for something, or someone, to change my mood that I didn't care if she thought I was a geek. It's pathetic, I know, but my heart soared when she waved back. I actually hoped she'd invite me in. *Sheesh, Sean, you are a jerk. It's pitch dark, five in the morning and you're hoping a middle-aged woman you've never even spoken to is going to invite you to join her for coffee. Yeah right, that's going to happen.*

Not surprisingly, there was no one at the desk in the hotel lobby. I left two quarters on the counter and took the last newspaper lying on the counter. It was yesterday's edition, but that didn't matter. Yesterday's news was better than no news at all, I figured.

As I walked back to the cabin I noticed that my neighbour was still standing at her window. We waved again.

I hadn't bothered locking the door when I left. There didn't seem to be much reason for concern about security. Who'd be around, way out here, at this hour? I threw the newspaper on the kitchen table and poured myself a mug of coffee even before I took off my jacket. A good cup of brew would make me feel better, I was sure.

But it didn't, not at all, and it was so cold in the cabin that I had to keep my jacket on and zipped closed the whole time I drank my coffee. Maybe I'd left the door open a bit when I went for the newspaper because the place was colder than ever. Finally, I couldn't sit there any longer so I picked up my coffee and took it up to the loft. I would read the paper under the warmth of the covers.

But I'd no sooner climbed into bed than I was sure I heard a weird, breathy voice call my name.

"Hello?" I called down the stairs, thinking that for some reason the woman next door had come in. But that didn't make any sense. Even if she had come in she couldn't have known my name. Thoroughly freaked out, I gathered every bit of courage I could muster and slowly made my way downstairs. Maybe there was a burglar. Leaving that door unlocked when I went to get the paper might have been a really dumb idea.

But the cabin was as empty as it should have been, so I went back upstairs, this time to have a warm shower. First, though, I dumped my suitcase out onto the bed. Then I could just rummage through all the gear I'd brought and decide what to wear and what to put away in the chest of drawers beside my bed.

The shower felt terrific. I stood letting the hot water pour over my body until I warmed up and then towelled off with the door closed to keep the heat in. When I opened the bathroom door, the drop in temperature actually made me gasp. *There has to be something the matter with this place. I'm going to have to move to a smaller chalet until the guys come at the end of the week.*

That change seemed even more important when I walked back into the bedroom because the pile of clothes I'd left out on the bed was gone. I tried to tell myself that I'd just thought about dumping the suitcase but that I really hadn't done it. I knew that wasn't true, though, and my clothes weren't on the bed anymore. They were back in my suitcase, and my suitcase was back on the floor.

In a panic, I dumped the suitcase out on the bed a second time. Then I wondered if being so cold and so tired was starting to make me lose my mind. I got dressed as fast as I could and ran for my car. By the time I hit the edge of town I'd settled down a bit, and I also realized that I was ravenously hungry. Fortunately, the first place I saw on the main street was a diner.

The warmth and the food smells that greeted me were more than welcome. Normally I'd have chosen a table in a far corner, but this time I sat myself down at the counter just to be near the only other human being in the place—the cook, I guessed.

A few minutes later he put a plate of bacon and eggs in front of me and asked, "What brings you into town so early?"

I surprised myself by describing the situation I'd just run from.

"Hmmmm," he said pulling on the strings of his grease-stained apron. "If you want my honest opinion here, I think you have a ghost."

"What? That's impossible," I shot back more vehemently than I intended to. "There's no such thing as ghosts."

"Have it your way then," he said, and walked away.

I went back to the chalet as soon as I'd finished eating; nothing about the place had improved. It was as unwelcoming as it had been when I'd fled from it earlier, maybe even worse, and it was definitely colder. That was the last straw. I headed upstairs to get my suitcase. I felt like a wimp, but I was going to have to ask management to put me into another chalet, at least until my friends got here. I wasn't going to spend another night in there—not alone, anyway.

When I got up to the bedroom, though, I was suddenly so tired that the thought of packing was absolutely overwhelming. Instead, I lay down on the unmade bed and immediately fell into a deep sleep. I woke up just plain confused. The curtains were closed so it was dark, and I had no idea what time it was or how long I'd slept. I grabbed my watch and fumbled for the bedside lamp. I'd been out of it for more than five hours! That was the longest I'd slept at one time since Boxing Day, and I'd done it in my clothes. I even still had my shoes on. I felt awful. I kicked off my shoes and rolled over. My head ached and my mouth tasted like last night's garbage. I wanted to sleep it off, whatever "it" was.

As I lay there, the noises downstairs started again. *Jeez,* I thought, *this place is enough to make a basket-case out of anyone.* I sat up. My head pounded. There were noises downstairs, definitely, but they sounded different than the ones I'd heard at night. These weren't scraping sounds. It sounded like there were a couple of people banging around down there. But that couldn't be. I'd locked the door. Hadn't I?

What if there was any chance that the cook at the diner this morning was right? What if there was a ghost in the place? "That's just dumb," I told myself out loud as I began to make my way to the staircase. Man it was cold. It had to be colder in here than it was outside! And the sounds kept up. They came from the living room.

Had it been my imagination, or was someone calling me again? And that awful wheezing sound—what was that? It was close. Almost beside me. It sounded human, like an old, sick person breathing.

"Don't go down there," the wheeze warned. I spun around. I was alone.

Then I heard one more bang—a familiar one. It was the front door closing.

I ran downstairs. The place was a mess, but it didn't look as though they'd taken anything. What a pair of idiots. Couldn't they figure the police would just follow their tracks? Jerks.

I picked up the phone to call the front desk, but the line had been cut. A shiver ran down my back. They'd planned to do more than steal. If I'd gone downstairs like I'd planned…

I ran next door. This time I didn't hesitate to introduce myself to the neighbour. "I need to use your phone," I told her, trying not to sound as upset as I felt.

She invited me to wait in her living room until the manager and then the police came. She even made me a cup of tea and did her best to make conversation.

"It was remarkable to see you walking with your mother yesterday," she said.

"Huh?"

"Remember? You were out walking so early. I figured it must have been your mother you were walking with. Of course, you'd have no way of knowing this, but she looks remarkably like Lillian Nelson used to. I still miss Lil. For years she and I rented side-by-side chalets during the week between Christmas and New Year's, but then she died about this time last year. That's the only reason the place was available for you to rent."

I could barely comprehend what I was hearing.

"Of course, Lil was a good age when she died. Amazing really, especially considering she'd been asthmatic for years. She dragged an oxygen bottle along with her everywhere she went. The darned thing scraped the floors up pretty good, and even so she wheezed like an old furnace, so she did. I've been missing her these last few days, I have to admit."

A strange light flashed through the woman's chalet.

"Well, there are the police now. You'd better go out and meet them."

I nodded and stumbled out of her house and toward the officers. It was hard to remember why I had called them.

210 Alberta Fireside Ghost Stories

Just a Trinket

"Mother, why would you buy such a silly thing?" Sally asked, making no attempt to hide her disdain for the strange, egg-shaped ornament on her mother's windowsill.

"You just mind your own business, young lady," the older woman scolded good-naturedly. "I thought it was interesting."

"What on earth is it?" the younger woman asked, picking up a small, garishly coloured china figurine.

"I don't rightly know exactly *what* it is, but it has my initials on it—see, right there on the bottom—it says MBR—for Mary Beth Roberts. I picked it up at the thrift shop in Athabasca. It's really nothing, just a trinket," her mother defended.

"Well, if it came from the thrift shop then I guess at least you didn't waste too much money getting it. You do know that it's just coincidence, the initials being the same as yours, right?"

"Of course I do, dear. Besides, I really don't think that how I spend my money should be any concern of yours."

Sally sighed and shook her head. Too often, visits with her mother deteriorated into bickering. After all these years she knew enough to leave at the first sign of tension. Bending to kiss her mother's cheek, she said, "I'd better get on my way now, Mother."

Watching her daughter walk away from the house, Mary Beth picked up the bright orange figurine and turned it over in her hands, smiling. Not because it was a pretty thing at all—far from it—but because how often do you find a knick-knack with your initials on it? Sally's opinion be damned.

She held the ornament in her lap as she looked out the window to the quiet neighbourhood where she'd lived for most of her adult life. The scene always soothed her, even with its inevitable changes over the years. At least, it had always soothed her before. Today, for some reason Mary Beth couldn't understand, the peacefulness outside irritated her.

Slipping the small ornament into her apron pocket, the woman got up to make herself a cup of tea. A nice warm cup of tea was bound to lift her spirits. She filled the kettle, set it on the stove to boil and took a tea bag out of the canister.

"Oh, hang the expense," she said out loud to herself, "I'm going to treat myself to two tea bags today."

Mary Beth was mildly surprised at the sound of her own voice. She definitely did sound aggravated. "That cranky Sally's disapproval is what's put me in this mood," she told herself as she waited for the kettle's whistle to sound. It was a sound she liked because she associated it with a warm drink and a break from whatever tasks she'd been doing. Today though, the kettle was silent for what seemed like an unusually long time, and the woman went back into the living room, reminding herself about watched pots not boiling.

She'd no sooner sat down than the whistle's shrill sound pierced her ears, startling her. Mary Beth jumped and ran to the kitchen, nonsensically talking to the kettle. "All right, all right, I'm coming," she snapped toward the stove before stopping dead in her tracks. "What's the matter with me? I'm really angry. I can hear it in my voice. This is silly."

She turned off the heat under the kettle and leaned against the counter long enough to take several deep breaths. A bad temper was something Mary Beth never could abide in anyone. To hear it coming out in herself was disconcerting. Finally, feeling more in control, she reached for the kettle, but as she began to pour the water, her arm gave a sudden twitch. Mary Beth screamed. She'd poured the boiling water all over her hand.

She hurried to the kitchen sink and ran cold water over the burn for as long as she could bear. The pain was intensifying. She needed to sit down. In agony, Mary Beth made her way back to the living room, clutching her hand against her chest, not wanting to see how badly she'd injured herself.

Finally, when the throbbing didn't subside, she forced herself to look at it. "Oh dear God," she uttered, shocked at the sight of the oozing, cracked, bright red skin. "I need to call Sally."

By the time the doctor had finished dressing the wound, Mary Beth was exhausted. Sally was concerned that the time might be approaching when her mother would have to give up her independence, but that was a discussion for another day. Her mother had been through enough this afternoon. For now it was enough just to be thankful that the accident hadn't been any worse than it was, and for the presence of her mother's long-standing neighbours. They would happily check in on her when Sally couldn't be there.

The painkillers the doctor had given Mary Beth assured that she slept through the night, and by the next morning her hand was feeling much more comfortable. Around mid-morning, kindly Mr. Sullivan from next door dropped in to see how she was doing. He made her a pot of tea and then, on his way out, admired the strange little figurine she'd picked up at the thrift shop the day before.

Yesterday seemed an eternity ago, what with burning herself, and by now she couldn't even recall what had attracted her to the ornament. Looking at the thing now, she had to agree with Sally—it was indeed a silly thing. "Do you like it?" she asked the man as he leaving. "Please take it then.

It's nothing, really. I picked it up in town yesterday, but now I wonder why I bothered. Please do take it. I'd be delighted if you did, really I would. It's just a trinket."

"If you're sure," the man replied hesitantly. "It's just that the colour is unusual. I think it's a dead match for my living room drapes."

"It's yours then, and thanks for checking in on me," Mary Beth said as she saw Mr. Sullivan to the door.

The moment he left, carrying the figurine with him, she had the strangest feeling of relief. It was almost as though she'd wrested back control of her life.

* * *

"What on earth is that?" Clara Sullivan asked as she saw what her husband had brought home with him from his visit next door.

"Just a trinket," the man said with a dismissive tone that he hoped would cover up the defensiveness he was feeling. He held the gift in his hand and looked at it admiringly. "Mrs. Roberts gave it to me. It caught my eye because it's the same shade as our drapes, and you know how that neighbour of ours is; she wanted to give me something to thank me for dropping in to see her. I'll just put it here on the table at the far side of my chair. That way you'll never even have to see it if you don't want to."

But the man needn't have bothered with the long explanation. His wife only heard "just a trinket" before going into the kitchen and turning on the radio. He sat down on his big easy chair and placed the ornament on the table beside him. Then he picked up the newspaper and lit his pipe, content to devote the rest of the morning to himself.

* * *

It was several hours before the fire started, but once it took hold, the flames engulfed the Sullivans' house in mere minutes. They were lucky to escape with their lives, but that was about all they escaped with. The house was gone completely. Even seasoned firefighters found the extent of the destruction virtually unbelievable, considering how quickly they were on it.

Police strung yellow tape around the perimeter of the smoldering ruins. Mary Beth, watching the commotion from her house, couldn't help but think how utterly cut off that bright plastic made her feel. She felt let down, even somehow guilty. Perhaps it was only because the excitement was over and the crowd that had gathered to watch the inferno had dispersed. Too bad there wasn't anything she could do to comfort the Sullivans. They'd be at his brother's house way over on the other side of town by now.

Sighing, Mary Beth put her head back to rest in her chair for a while, so she didn't see the teenaged girls poking through the rubble that only hours before had been her next door neighbours' home.

"What did you find?" the blonde girl asked her friend.

"Just this," the other girl replied, holding out her hand to reveal an odd china figurine with blotches of orange painted on one side and the initials MBR printed on another. "I'm going to give it to my aunt. She teaches geometry so she loves different shapes, and an egg shape is her favourite."

"But what is it?"

"I don't know. Just a trinket, I guess."

The Pilot's Life (and Death)

Sheila mumbled a response that she hoped disguised her sigh of exasperation. Her pilot for the flight was a very talkative guy, that much was for sure. The day-long meeting she'd endured had left her longing for complete silence during the trip, but apparently that was not going to happen.

The private flight was a thank-you present from her boss—an extravagant demonstration of his appreciation for all she'd done to land the contract. Ironically, now it would seem that his thank-you gift to her was going to make the short trip by air from Red Deer to Medicine Hat an endurance test.

The pilot might feel the necessity to talk, but she felt absolutely no obligation to listen to him. She looked out the window and let her mind wander, consoling herself with the knowledge that this charter was definitely the quickest, and therefore the best, way to get home. Listening to the pilot's babble was a small price to pay for that reward.

Sheila appreciated the expense her boss had gone to in booking the flight. She definitely wanted to get home to spend as much of the weekend as possible with Scott because she was excited. She had just found out that in just a few months he would be a father, and she couldn't wait to tell him.

Just as she thought the word "father" she heard it too, and the coincidence of timing yanked her awareness back into the small plane.

"Yeah, a lot of people don't believe me when I tell them that, but honestly, I did start flying as a kid. My father was a pilot. He owned a small plane and for my 10th birthday, he took me flying. He flew out of an old airstrip just south of here. We did a few "touch and goes" and then he let me have the controls. I'll never forget that. You know, I guess my father was my best friend. He died a few years ago. I still miss him."

Sheila turned toward the man and nodded tentatively, knowing that a larger motion would have aggravated the throbbing tension headache building behind her eyes.

"It's a bit weird that my father is on my mind so much this afternoon. It's probably just because I associate my dad with this area. I hope my chatter isn't disturbing you."

The man shifted in his seat and rubbed his eyes. Sheila noticed the sweat on his face had created a film of moisture. She wondered if he was aware.

"Say, Sheila—you don't mind if I call you by your first name, do you?" he asked, but didn't pause to give her a chance to reply. "You wouldn't happen to have any antacid tablets with you? I could sure use one. Got terrible heartburn for some reason."

Sheila fished in her briefcase until she came to the roll of Tums she kept there for emergencies. "One or two?" she asked.

"It's getting bad. Two for sure. No wait, can you spare more, please? I'll replace them for you as soon as we're on the ground."

His voice had developed a shakiness to it that concerned Sheila. She held the unopened package toward the man. He shook his head and mumbled something about not being able to open it himself. She ran her thumbnail across the folded foil, loosening the wrap. The pilot nodded slowly but didn't make a move to take any of the tablets. His head was turned away from her, out the window to his left.

"Dad! What are you doing here?" he said, slurring his words.

This dude's beginning to worry me, Sheila thought. "Hey!" she yelled. "Focus, would you please?"

"It's getting worse," he said, slurring his words. "You gotta take over. Land this thing, will you?"

Sheila grabbed his shoulder and shook him. "Are you crazy? I can't fly a plane! What's wrong? Are you hallucinating? You're supposed to be flying this plane, remember? You can have your daydreams on someone else's dime."

But his lifeless body slumped forward in his safety harness.

Sheila swore. She was terrified. The plane tilted to the right as it lost altitude faster than she would have believed possible.

"I'm gonna die. In seconds. Pregnant. In a plane crash. Seconds from now," she whimpered. Somehow not screaming felt important, and she pulled herself together. She might be about to die, but she'd do it with dignity.

Serenity infused the cockpit. Resigned, Sheila watched as the ground rushed up to meet her. Bile rising in her throat, she braced for the inevitable end, but at the last second, she felt the nose of the plane tilt up. As it flew across the field she could hear the top of corn stalks brushing against the undercarriage, and then the scratching ceased and she saw a clearing in front of her. The plane touched down, then rolled almost to the end of the clearing before coming to a stop, and the engine came to idle.

Sheila snapped open her seat belt and got out of the plane. As she stood looking around at the long clearing surrounded by cornfields, she realized that she was standing on a cracked and broken runway—the mere ghost of a long-abandoned air strip.

Dying to be Home

Violet Nickerson had one last request: she didn't want to die in the hospital. It wasn't so much that she wanted the comfort of being in her home as it was that she'd heard that the old St. Michael's Hospital in her hometown of Lethbridge was haunted by the ghost of a nun, and the story had always terrified her. Violet's husband George was, of course, making every effort to make sure his dear wife's final hours were no less horrible than they absolutely had to be. Toward that end he'd hired a private duty nurse, but also, for the most part, he stayed right beside the dying woman.

One afternoon, George excused himself from his wife's room to fix himself a sandwich for lunch. Chewing on the tasteless concoction, he wandered from the kitchen into the living room and looked out the front window. There, coming up the walk, was a nun. George cursed and vowed not to answer the door. A visit from some religious person was the last thing he needed at the moment.

Just then Violet's nurse hurried toward him and somberly announced, "I'm sorry, Mr. Nickerson, your wife's gone."

George looked out the front window. The nun was nowhere to be seen.

A Haunting Melody

Monday, June 1; afternoon

It's so good to finally be here at the lodge in Cold Lake. Even just driving out of the city helped. Honestly, I could feel the tension and strain easing with each kilometre I put between me and that wretched school. Teaching junior high must be the devil's own punishment. I can't imagine what I've ever done to deserve the torture that career provides. The only benefit, aside from the pretty respectable wage I earn, has been that all the training to teach Language Arts has given me the ability to express myself more than adequately, which is one of the reasons I've brought this diary with me. I hope to write a bit in it everyday. If I can get into the habit, I'm hoping I'll end up with a decent memoir. Then all I have to do is get a publisher for it. Of course, there's no guarantee I'll make enough to support myself, but Frank McCourt and Elizabeth Gilbert certainly did all right.

Thank goodness the drive here wasn't too stressful because the first thing the desk clerk said when I got to the hotel was that I couldn't have the room I usually get when I stay here. Instead they gave me this corner room. It's quite a bit bigger and they said I could have it for the same price as the other one, so it turned out all right, but I do like my regular room so initially I wasn't very pleased.

This room's more like a suite really, plus it has two large windows; they're at right angles to one another. I think that's kind of unusual and yet oddly familiar at the same time. Anyway, the end result is that the light in the room is very interesting. I think it'll be good for my painting. I've only brought the acrylics with me, which in a way is a shame because the water colours would've been wonderful, but I'm only here for a few days and I must remember that I am supposed to be resting. Last time when everything became too much for me and I stayed here for a spell, I think I delayed my recovery by pushing too hard. Lesson learned. And that's another reason to be grateful for this new room they've put me in. I won't be quite so reminded of how drained I was when I stayed here just two years ago. I'm definitely not nearly as burned out now as I was then.

Something else that makes this room nicer than the one I've had before is the lovely music. It's so soft and quiet that I can barely hear it, but still, it's there in the room and quite soothing.

Judging by the menus I've seen, the meals here look as though they're going to be as good as ever, and the wooden staircase down to the lake has been repaired so I'm looking forward to long walks on the beach. I'll take my sketchbook to the lake, and maybe even the small easel I brought with me.

This little holiday is going to be exactly the break I need. How I wish I didn't ever have to go back to teaching. If only I could support myself another way—maybe the memoir writing will work out, and then there's my art too.

For now though, just getting away like this helps so much. The music in this room—it's odd—very lovely, but odd. It's almost as though the sounds are part of the essence of the room. The view from these windows is so calming.

Monday evening

It's been a lovely day. I feel so much better already, and it crossed my mind that I might not have to live on royalties from just a book of memoirs. I've missed an obvious possibility.

Given that I can write *and* paint, I should create a series of children's books. Coming here for a few days was such a good idea; I'm already thinking far more clearly and creatively than I ever was before.

Tuesday, June 2

I've finally remembered where I'd seen windows like the ones in this room—big ones, positioned at right angles to each other. It was last winter, in that couple's house, the ones who hosted the staff Christmas party. There were windows like this in their den. Their party was a bit much, I thought, but I did love that one room in their house, and the windows in this room put me in mind of that. It seemed to be a room where a man could relax completely, and that's just what I intend to do here. I haven't been able to paint yet, but that's all right. I have another six days.

That music is still playing somewhere in the background. It's quite lovely, but it's so indistinct that for the life of me I can't make out where it's coming from or even whether it's an orchestra or choral music. It's a little frustrating not to know. I asked at the front desk, but the woman there didn't seem to know what I was talking about. Odd.

Wednesday, June 3

I still haven't been able to paint at all. Truth be told, when I'm in the room I tend to spend a lot of my time listening to the music. Maybe listening *for* the music would be a better way to phrase it because the sound is so subtle.

I have been going for lots of walks along the beach, mostly because it's the only way to get clear of the music in this room—if you can call it music. I guess they're wind chimes

I'm hearing, but they're not the little tinny ones that everyone had years ago. They'd have to be those lovely, long wooden tubes being blown ever so gently against a heavily covered hammer. It's a mellow ringing, and it seems to haunt the room. I do wish, though, that I could either hear it properly or find a way to silence it.

The front desk clerk doesn't believe me, I'm sure, but she did send two people from the hotel's maintenance department to check the room. It didn't matter; neither one could even hear it. Of course, that really shouldn't be surprising. After all, what can you expect from such uncouth creatures? They're likely deaf to any music other than the wretched cacophony that's become so popular on the radio these days.

I'm beginning to wonder if those big corner windows are safe. I don't really think they are because surely having them so close together would weaken the walls at that edge. I'd actually insist that they change my room except that I'm only staying for a few more days. Besides, I'm toying with the idea of going home on Saturday so that I can go into work for a few hours on Sunday. That way on Monday when the other teachers—to say nothing of those little urchins who make up the student body—come in I'll already feel back in the saddle.

I must get out of this room again. There's no place else to go except to the lake. My walks by the water have been good, even though it's a rocky beach and I can't really get much of a pace going for fear of turning an ankle.

Thursday, June 4

I still haven't painted as much as a brush stroke. I spend most of my time just sitting by the lake because frankly, those windows have become a serious worry. The wall just can't be as strong there as it should be.

And that infernal music! It's really getting to be more than I can bear. I think I'm hearing the same melody over and over again. The hotel's owners are being utter block-heads about it too, though they have called in an electrician, I'll give them that much. But when the man came to inspect the room he couldn't find anything wrong anywhere in the room. He couldn't hear anything either.

Well, I've paid to stay here until Saturday so I shall, but honestly, I don't know if it's safe here any longer. Between those windows and that music I just feel much more secure down by the lake. I've never much liked a rocky beach before, but this one's intriguing. I'd go so far as to say compelling. More's the pity that I've come late to that party, so to speak, because I seem to be becoming quite the rock hound. I really enjoy examining them and choosing some to keep. A few times I've been so weighted down from rocks in my pockets that it's been tough to get up that long wooden staircase.

Friday, June 5

I'm so uncomfortable here. If it weren't for the thought of that terrible drive back to the city, I'd leave right away. I can feel the tension and strain building. If only they'd given me my usual room. The light in this one is so strange, but that's no wonder considering those oddly placed, overly large windows. It's criminal that they've charged me the same rate for this room when it's actually dangerous to stay here. Why did I even bother to bring any paints with me? I haven't been able to even move a brush. Perhaps if I could've painted then I might have been able to get well, but when I'm inside it's almost impossible to concentrate on anything but the music—well that and checking the weakened wall in the corner of the room to make sure it's going to hold through the night. Aside from that I'm spending as much time as possible on the rocky beach. Each time I go to the lake I pick up more and more stones. Having the rocks close to me seems to help. It's a wonder the pockets in my clothes haven't given way.

Every employee at the hotel must be in on the secret of the music in this room. Even the lowliest yard workers claim not to be able to hear the damnable chimes when they come into my room, despite the fact that the ringing is quite clear and loud by now. I've tried to assure them that they don't have to be loyal to their employer about this, that I'll never tell anyone that they admit they can hear it—which obviously they must—but still they stubbornly toe to the company line.

This morning I'm going to have to vary my walk route a bit. I'll take my rock collection with me, I think. It seems only right to return the stones to the lake. They won't all fit in my pockets no matter how many clothes I wear, so I'll put the rest in my backpack and strap it on. Instead of walking alongside the lake as I have been doing, I think this time I'll walk out into the lake for a change. The water will be refreshing, and if I go in deep enough it should muffle the sound of the music. Such relief…

Revenge of the Wronged

Len was devastated when the transmission on his car broke down. He liked his job as a shipper at a warehouse in Calgary's northeast, but after deductions he barely cleared enough to cover his day-to-day expenses. There was no way his pay would stretch far enough to cover the cost of a major car repair, and summer was just around the corner. The thought of having to ride back and forth to work in a smelly old bus appalled him almost as much as the realization that without a car he wouldn't be able to get out to the lake on weekends. His summer would be ruined.

Fortunately, the first week in July means the opening of the Calgary Stampede—a time when temporary jobs in the city are thick on the ground. Just 10 days of moonlighting, and Len would have the money he needed to get his car repaired, probably with some left over for extra spending money. Smiling to himself, he made his way down to the hiring office on the Stampede Grounds. The job postings board was full of listings, but the more Len scanned them the less he was smiling. It hadn't occurred to him that the toughest, least desirable jobs would pay the highest hourly rates—but that was clearly the case.

No such thing as easy money, he told himself with a sigh. Getting his car running was desperately important to him, though, so he committed himself to the dirtiest job on the grounds—stable hand. He consoled himself with the fact that he'd only be at it for two weeks, and even then only evenings and weekends. He also vowed not to tell anyone he knew that he'd been forced to shovel manure just to get his car fixed.

I'll just park my personality at the door of the stable and do the work each night, he thought. *That way there's no chance I'll get talking to someone and find out we know some of the same people or anything like that.*

Initially, Len's plan worked well, although he did realize that his co-workers were beginning to talk amongst themselves about how unfriendly he was. Frankly, he didn't much care if he offended a few people—well, except for one grizzled old man who actually seemed to be hurt by Len's unsocial attitude. He hadn't intended to be offensive, especially as he admired the guy's strength and stamina.

By break time on the third night, Len felt badly enough about the older man's reaction that he offered to buy him a coffee. Once they each had a cup in their hands, the two perched themselves on a fence rail outside the stables.

"Thanks for the brew, son," the old man said to Len.

"You're welcome. I just wanted to tell you that I'm not snobby, and it's not that I don't think you're a nice guy. That has nothing to do with me not being very friendly. It's just that I'm only here to earn some extra cash as quick as I can."

The old-timer stared silently at the steam rising from the foam cup he held between his gnarled hands. When he spoke, his voice was so quiet that Len had to lean forward to hear him. "I thought that might be it. It wasn't more than a dozen years ago that I was pretty much where you are right now—desperate to earn some extra cash fast. Of course, I didn't choose my method of acquiring that cash quite as wisely as you've done."

The man spit on the dirt beside his feet before he continued. "Truth be told, I don't mind a quiet man; as a matter of fact, I even admire quiet, but frankly I don't much like the idea of sitting here in silence for 15 minutes or so. You told me your story, and now, if it's all right with you, I'd like to tell you mine."

Len nodded, watching the man out of the corner of his eye. *The guy has to be in his seventies,* Len thought. *He must have some kind of amazing story.*

The man took a gulp of his coffee, swished it around in his mouth, swallowed and then began to speak. "First of all, I should tell you that I'm not nearly as old as I look. Not that long ago I was actually a pretty good-looking guy."

Len looked at his companion and wondered if the man was pulling his leg, but there was nothing in the man's expression to indicate any teasing. *If he's younger than he looks then that would explain how strong he is,* Len thought.

"Not so many years ago I found myself just like you are now—in a real tight place for money. Now I don't know what's caused your shortfall and I won't ask. In return for that courtesy I don't expect any questions from you."

Len nodded, surprised at how good it felt to know that someone not only understood but actually respected his situation.

"It happened when I was working in a hospital. I didn't have a big position or anything, just an orderly. The job didn't pay much but it was secure, which is more than I can say for a few other parts of my life, and that's how I came to need some extra cash, fast. See, a few of the guys I hung out with were not exactly what you'd call straight-up characters. So then add that to the fact that working around corpses as much as I did—well—let's just say that death had lost its delicacy for me."

Len shivered in the warm night. The man's story had drawn him in. He'd never seen a dead body, nor did he ever want to.

The man crushed his empty coffee cup before before continuing. "By that point in my life, if I'd learned anything it was that there's always a market for gruesome stuff. So when one of my buddies offered me five thousand dollars to swipe a skull from the morgue, I mighta been a bit surprised, but I sure wasn't shocked—especially not coming from this particular guy. He was an odd kind, always active, always into some new scheme or another, working the angles. Made a good living at it too. Seems he knew some rich guy who liked having really freakish ornaments in his house and was willing to pay top dollar. Well, didn't that just fit in with my predicament?"

The sun, a bright red ball of fire, was sinking slowly behind the foothills, and it was nearly time for the two men to return to work. Clearly there was more to his companion's story, but perhaps the man was just going to let it ride on implication. Len was about to suggest that they get back to work when the man started to talk again.

"It didn't take long before I had a chance to get my hands on a skull. It was from the body of a homeless man. No one claimed his remains, and the medical students had already cut him up pretty good, so the mortician didn't question the fact that I delivered a headless cadaver to him. I slipped the skull into my lunch bucket."

"A human skull fit into your lunch bucket?" Len squirmed at the thought.

"You'd be surprised how small a skull actually is," the man laughed mirthlessly. "Either that or you'd be surprised at how big my lunch bucket was."

Len didn't know whether the old man was kidding or not. Nor did he want to ask. He also didn't know if he could stomach hearing the rest of the old man's story.

"That evening I took the skull to my friend. He had the money for me there and then, in cash. An hour later I was free of my financial obligation. I tell you, I slept like a baby that night. Next day I heard that my friend had been in an accident. He'd been on his way to deliver the skull. At first the accident didn't seem to be that big a deal; the skull wasn't even damaged. But nothing's gone right for my friend since then. For one thing, his back's been so sore ever since that he hasn't been able to hold a job. Doctors couldn't find anything specific wrong, so they couldn't help him. He took to drinking pretty heavily to ease the pain. He used to be quite the high roller, but now he lives in a moth-eaten room downtown. I used to try to visit him, but seeing him like that just got too depressing, so I quit."

A jet flew low overhead, startling Len so much that he lost his balance and spilled what was left of his coffee on his jeans.

"I've upset you, haven't I, young fella? Well, don't worry," the man continued. "The story's nearly finished because, you see, by the time I woke up that next morning I'd aged more than 20 years."

Len took a deep breath. Slowly, his voice barely a whisper, he asked, "And the guy who bought the skull? What happened to him?"

"You know, I've never been sure. I do have my suspicions. Do you remember that big fire that ripped through a mansion toward the west of town? The guy had a house full of weird stuff, things he shouldn't have had, like native medicine bundles, elephant tusks, that sort of thing."

"I think I read about that in the newspaper. Was that the guy who tried putting out the fire with his bare hands so that he wouldn't have to call the fire department?" Len asked.

"The same," the old man answered. "His hands were so badly burned that they had to be amputated. I understand he's been in a psychiatric hospital ever since. Of course, I don't know for certain it's the same guy, and I'm not about to put any effort into finding out. All I know is that I've been old ever since, and I think I got off easy."

A Stranger Conversation

Carol sat at her favourite picnic bench in Calgary's Riley Park. She had a magazine open in front of her, but none of the articles held her interest quite as much as the street theatre going on around her was. Dozens of teenagers and 20-somethings were enjoying themselves jogging, biking, roller blading and playing Frisbee on the lush, green expanse of grass. She found the youngsters' antics vastly more entertaining than anything in her copy of *Canadian Living*.

She was thoroughly enjoying her solitude when a well-dressed, bespectacled, middle-aged man seemed to appear out of nowhere. Silently, he sat down across from Carol at the picnic table. He didn't as much as offer a nod in her direction, or even make eye contact with her. He merely took a book out of his jacket pocket and began reading.

At first she was relieved that he wasn't going to intrude on her privacy, but a few moments later she began to feel somewhat offended by the combination of his barging in on her and then ignoring her existence. *What's up with that?* she wondered, cleared her throat and, looking for a little revenge against his rudeness, interrupted the man by asking if he was enjoying book he was reading.

"Why yes, yes I am enjoying it, as a matter of fact. Thank you for asking," he replied.

"What's it about?" Carol persisted.

"It's a ghost story," the man told her. "And a very good one at that, very spooky and atmospheric. It really gets you thinking."

"You believe in ghosts then, do you?" Carol's interest was truly piqued now.

"I do believe in ghosts, yes. I believe that ghosts are everywhere, that they're around us all the time," he answered.

"There's no such thing as ghosts," she responded scornfully and in no uncertain terms.

"Is that right?" the man asked, just as he and his book suddenly vanished before Carol's eyes.

The End